Property Sourcing Compliance: Keeping You on the Right Side of the Law

Tina Walsh

For my husband Tony without whom this book would never have been completed, thank you for your constant love, support, encouragement and unfailing belief in me x

Book Reviews

John Paul

"Just wow; it's not very often I read a book that holds my interest as much as this did. As a businessman with a property sourcing company I took special interest in this book and I was not disappointed. I don't mind telling you that I'm going to be implementing some of the advice in the book into my business immediately. Tina's grasp of legislation and compliance is first rate and if you follow this book then you will not fall short. Whether you are a property sourcer or an investor you NEED this book in your life – not to do so is foolish. Well done, Tina."

John Paul – Managing Director, The Castledene Group

Sarah Poynton-Ryan

"Tina has successfully achieved simplicity from the often-misunderstood chaos of property sourcing compliance. Easy to read and understand! An absolute must if a sustainable sourcing business is what you desire."

Sarah Poynton-Ryan – Rent Guaranteed UK

Rob Stewart

"Even as an experienced property professional, Tina has opened my eyes to potential risks involved with property sourcing that no one else in the industry covers. Written in an easy-to-read, step-by-step process, this book is essential reading for all property sourcers and investors."

Rob Stewart – Investor, Entrepreneur & Speaker –
The Property Education Group

Justin Whittemore

"Tina's book is a pleasure to read. A topic that could have be very wooden and dull has been turned into an easy-to-understand quick-start guide that I believe all sourcers, and all investors that plan to buy from sourcers, must read before getting started. Thank you, Tina, for your efforts towards raising the standards in our industry."

Justin Whittemore – Professional Property Investor,
Trainer & Mentor

Daniel Latto

"I have known Tina for a number of years; in fact I was her mentor at the beginning when she started her sourcing business. Tina has clearly dug deep on researching this book, which is written in a way that is easy to digest. So whether you are an investor or you source property, you need this book – READ IT"

Daniel Latto – Business & Property Coach

Kevin Wright

"If you are in, or intend to get into property sourcing, Tina Walsh's book is a must read. Getting it wrong when you are sourcing a high-value commodity like property can land you in serious hot water. If you subscribe to the 'better safe than sorry' mindset, buy Tina's book, read, understand and act on it."

Kevin Wright – Finance Consultant & Property Investor
Awards Judge 2016

John Corey

"Are you a professional or a lazy impostor pretending to source 'deals' for others? Do you understand the legal obligations? Know Your Client & Anti-Money Laundering? Tina has captured 'best practice'. Rise above the noise and join the professionals; buy, read and apply Tina's insights."

John Corey – Property Fortress

Alex Matts

"Tina, 'The Queen of Compliance', is without doubt a subject-matter expert. The content in this book is invaluable, not just to those who are just starting out in sourcing and trading properties, but those that have already established businesses. Ignorance is not an excuse in the eyes of the law.

Also for those property investors that use sourcers to be sure they are dealing with compliant professionals that have everyone's best interest at heart.

This can be a heavy subject, but the author's intrinsic knowledge has enabled her to present this vital information in a reader-friendly format. A great read that will become the 'go-to reference' in years to come."

Alex Matts – Property and Investment Specialist

Acknowledgements

Firstly, a special thanks goes to everyone that has been involved in the creation and launch of this book, without whom it would never have been finished. Stephanie Hale's knowledge, experience, support and encouragement throughout the entire process have been invaluable; saying "thank you" just doesn't seem enough.

Over the past 6 years of my professional property journey many people have had a huge influence on how my company is structured and the high standards to which it operates today, others have had a profound affect on me, so I am taking this opportunity to say a huge and heartfelt "thank you" to each and every one of you.

Kevin Green and the Kevin Green Wealth (KGW) Team

Without Kevin and the KGW Team, I would not have enjoyed the success that I have to date nor would I have the ability to be able to look forward and recognise all that I could be in the future. Kevin and his team's wide-ranging business experience, encouragement, support, and guidance have been invaluable to my success.

www.kevingreen.co.uk

Daniel Latto

Saying thank you to Dan really doesn't cover how much I owe him. It was Dan that worked with Tony & I in the early days, *'eeking'* out of us what we were passionate about, what type of business might work, setting our goals and listening to the excuses as to why we hadn't done something! His ability to develop and build businesses as well as having a unique ability to change mindsets is nothing short of amazing!

https://daniellatto.co.uk/

Sue Elkington

What can I say about Sue, she is the loveliest lady that you could ever wish to meet. She genuinely wants to help people and has a heart of gold. Sue's depth of knowledge about refurbishment is nothing short of amazing. She is passionate about refurbishment and completing her projects not only to the highest standards but also just as myself compliantly and within regulations. I am privileged to be able to call her a friend.

Mark I'Anson

Mark believed in me even when at times I had lost faith in myself. He encouraged me to find my own niche within the property sector and no matter how grim things could look at times, to never give up on my dream. For your continued help and support, I send my heartfelt thanks.

Alex Matts

I have lost track of the number of Facebook messages, emails and texts that I have sent at all hours of the day to Alex, asking for his advice on a current development or commercial project. At a time when I was learning (yes, I know that will never stop Alex), he always had time for me, to answer my questions and reassure me that I was on the right track. This is my opportunity to say, "Thank you," but not just at the bottom of an email!

Marc Stokes-Denson

It feels as if I have known Marc all of my life. From when we first met we 'got on' really well and I did not hesitate when he suggested that we could work together on some projects. Marc quickly realised that 'figures' were definitely not my forte but he spent the time with me to help improve my skills. He opened my eyes to the possibilities that larger projects hold and his skill set of assessing and managing a project are awesome. I would not be where I am today if it were not for marc's friendship and ongoing support; I look forward to working with him on future exciting projects!

Rob Stewart & John Paul (Property Education Group)

Rob's easygoing and approachable personality is a ray of light in the property-training sector. His insight into systemising your business for sustained growth from the start has been invaluable to me. His approach to training and ability to cut to the chase with what has to be done, simplifying the whole process is awesome!

John's passion for building a company where your staff are key to your success is a subject that should be taught more widely than is currently the case. When building my business, I will always look back at John's advice, and if I can emulate even 50% of what John has achieved in his company, I will truly have reached high standards in staff recruitment, employment, retention, and development.

http://thepropertyeducationgroup.com/

Justin Whittemore & Mark Beal (Intelligent Property Academy - IPA)

Whilst I haven't known Justin and Mark that long they have left a long lasting impression on me. Together they share a huge passion for the Rent-to-Rent and Serviced Accommodation sector and have an immense, unsurpassed knowledge. Their willingness to share that knowledge and experience through their high-quality training courses provides a 'breath of fresh air' approach in the training sector.

http://www.i-propertyacademy.co.uk/

Ross Mallalieu (The 'Agent Whisperer' - Intelligent Property Academy - IPA)

Thank you to Ross for his enthusiastic insights into dealing with agents, how to approach, speak to and build professional relationships with them. Working with him always made me smile, and he is very deserving of his nickname 'The Agent Whisperer".

http://www.i-propertyacademy.co.uk/

Sarah Poynton-Ryan (Package 4 Profit - Intelligent Property Academy - IPA)

Thank you to Sarah for giving me the opportunity to stand alongside her on stage and talk to audiences about Property Sourcing Compliance. Sarah is a passionate believer in training to raise standards in our industry and working with her and the IPA team is always great fun and an absolute pleasure and privilege.

www.rentguaranteed.uk

Neil Larkin

Neil is a genuine, down to earth, lovely guy. His long-term dream of helping others to achieve success through investing in property is what drives him forward every day. Neil is a 'giver' and will chat for hours about one of his passions in life, property investment, acquiring assets and cash flow. A huge "thank you" for your encouragement, support, and ongoing belief in what Tony & I are trying to achieve over the next 5 - 10 years. Tony & I look forward to working with you on many projects in the years to come.

John Corey

A huge thank you to John for sharing his expert knowledge in the areas of sourcing JV finance and investment deal marketing compliance. Like myself, John is passionate about compliance and raising standards across our industry.

http://www.propertyfortress.com/

Foreword

Whether you are a property sourcer, deal packager, an experienced investor or completely new to the sector, this book is a must read. Tina passes on her extensive knowledge gained over more than five years of intensive study, whilst working only part-time as a well respected, professional property sourcer in her own right.

The property investment sector, as we know it has changed significantly over the past couple of years. We have seen increases in stamp duty and landlord tax liability, introduction of the Immigration Act 2016, changes to HMO regulations, EPC certificates and also not forgetting the roll out of Universal Credit and the Construction, Design and Management Regulations 2015.

With our sector increasingly coming under intense scrutiny, not just the landlords but also the "we buy anything for cash within 24 hours" brigade, how much longer before the whole property sourcing sector, good, bad, or indifferent is put under the spotlight? The majority of property sourcers or deal packagers are either completely ignorant of the Legislation and Regulations, vaguely know about them but choose to ignore them or are fully aware but refuse to be compliant.

Just taking into consideration Anti-Money Laundering, it is believed that in excess of £36 billion is laundered through the UK every year, and one of the main areas targeted by criminal gangs and terrorist groups is the property sector. When you digest this information, you can begin to understand the need for having a good understanding of the relevant laws. If you are found to be in breach of these regulations, then you could face an unlimited fine or even imprisonment.

Tina covers every stage required for you to set up and run your property sourcing business, but more importantly to set it up to be fully compliant. She takes Legislation and Regulation and turns it into an easy read, step-by-step process that anyone can follow.

With Tina's fundamental knowledge and understanding of the sector, this book will ensure that property sourcers across England and Wales have a working knowledge of Legislation and Regulation whilst fully understanding their responsibilities towards a vendor or investor. Remember, "Ignorance is no defence in law".

Kevin Green
As seen on Channel 4's T.V programme 'The Secret Millionaire'
www.kevingreen.co.uk

About the Author

"Tina takes Legislation and Regulation and turns it into an easy read, step-by-step process that anyone can follow..."

(Kevin Green – As seen on Channel 4's T.V programme, 'The Secret Millionaire'*)*

For as long as she can remember, Tina was interested in the law. She joined the Lancashire Constabulary Police Service at the age of 16 years, becoming a fully-fledged Woman Police Constable at the age of 18 ½ years and going on to serve for over 14 years in East Lancashire.

Throughout her career as a police officer, Tina never knew from one day to the next what situations she would have to face and deal with. From juvenile nuisance to fatal road traffic accidents, her days were varied and certainly never dull. But, one incident will always stand out, and whenever she thinks about it, the adrenalin always kicks in again:

In late November 1993, Tina was working in Burnley, and on this particular day covering an area on Mobile Patrol. That day she was working an early shift, 6 a.m. to 2 p.m., and at the beginning of the shift had another policewoman in the vehicle with her as passenger; they had arranged to cross over onto another mobile patrol area to carry out some enquiries, and during that time another patrol car with two male colleagues onboard, would cover for them.

Having completed their enquiry, Tina and her colleague were just getting back into their police vehicle to return to their own area when a call came over the radio from their central communications room:

"... Report of an armed robbery in progress Stoneyholme Post Office Burnley, requesting patrols to attend ..." Tina's colleague responded, "... Panda 1 attending, ETA 4 minutes ..." The patrol with their male colleagues (Panda 2) did the same.

Tina and her colleague set off, blue lights and sirens blaring, they had a main road to cross in peak time morning traffic. Suddenly a call came over the radio system, "Urgent assistance required, shots fired, officer down, ambulance needed." Tina was just around the corner, her colleague responded, " ETA 30 seconds."

As Tina pulled around the corner to the scene, the other patrol car (Panda 2) was stopped at the side of the road, neither car door open, and she could not she see either of her colleagues. A masked male was walking away from the front of the car, carrying a sawn-off shotgun and was making his way towards the now visible 'getaway' car, three other occupants visible. Tina screeched her car to a halt behind the other patrol car but dead centre in the road. The armed masked man turned to face Tina and her colleague. He turned away from the 'getaway car' and began to walk towards them, raising the shotgun up to waist height, both hands on the gun, right hand on the trigger of the gun that had already shot at least one colleague.

The masked, armed robber stopped in front of her vehicle. He stood, legs slightly apart with the shotgun tucked to his right-hand side, finger still on the trigger and stared directly at Tina for what seemed like an eternity. After 15 or 20 seconds, the masked man began to back away towards the 'getaway' car, still pointing the shotgun at them. He got into the car, and it sped off at very high speed down a side street.

Tina quickly pulled alongside the other patrol car to check her colleagues. Her colleague in the passenger seat waved for Tina to leave them and pursue the 'armed gang'. Tina set off to try to catch up with them.

Tina caught glimpses of the getaway car, as they sped through built up areas at terrifying speeds. Eventually, she rounded a corner and spotted the 'getaway' car abandoned at the side of the road, all of the doors were open, and a man was standing on the pavement, obviously in shock; they had taken his car from him at gunpoint and made off.

That was the end of Tina's participation in the pursuit, details of the new car were passed to other patrols, and she remained at the scene with the original getaway car to protect any evidence.

Whilst un-injured herself, this was an experience that she will never forget.

Following a further two years' dedicated service, Tina retired in July 1995 following an injury received whilst on duty, which caused permanent nerve damage to her right arm. The injury was obtained struggling to arrest a young woman who had caused damage to the glass panel in a door of a local public house, Tina removing her to ensure the safety of the other members of the public.

It was during her service in the police force that her passion for the law and compliance blossomed. Privately, she and her husband, Tony had always risen up the property ladder by buying, renovating, moving in and then selling. In 2005, they decided that it would be a good idea to make the step up to owning their own home as well as a separate property to let out for extra income, which in principle was a good idea. Although, without any knowledge, making the rooky mistake of buying two separate properties (townhouse and apartment), new build, off plan, from a local development wasn't the best idea. Whilst believed to be 'good buys', in reality looking back, with only a 10% discount on the purchase price, they were actually a pretty poor deal.

They had expected to live in the townhouse for 18 months and then sell, but to continue to hold onto the apartment for the extra income. In reality, with the market crash in 2007, they couldn't sell the townhouse so decided to stay there and sell the apartment instead, as the return on investment was poor, less than 4% gross. The sale of the apartment just about covered the cost of purchase and set up. This error in judgment somewhat curbed her enthusiasm to try again.

After spending several years self-employed and then in the healthcare sector, her interest in the property sector again came to the fore when in 2011 she met Kevin Green and it was suggested that she look into property sourcing as a sector to start a business in; which, since leaving the police force, was what she had really wanted to do.

In October 2012, Sanctuary Property Sourcing Ltd was founded. Tina spent the first 10 months researching and networking to build up knowledge and contacts whilst creating a legal and compliant platform that soon became an established, professional, and highly regarded property sourcing business, providing investors with a bespoke service throughout the North West. Their clients range from individuals looking for a single Buy to Let investment, through building up portfolios, HMO's and commercial conversions to healthcare companies wanting 40+ acre sites for bespoke, modern care facilities.

Sadly, property sourcing appears to have amassed an impression in some quarters that it is run by amateurs, carrying out 'dodgy deals', with very little knowledge and providing unsuspecting investors with a poor quality service.

Whilst property sourcing is something that she and now Tony, since his recent retirement from the police force, enjoy together, Tina had always wanted to expand into the training sector, to be able to share her passion for property sourcing legality and compliance; a knowledge that has taken over five years to amass, allowing others to work to the same high standards.

Tina's aim is to increase awareness, knowledge, and professionalism within the sourcing sector, sharing her immense knowledge on compliance with budding new sourcers or established businesses so that eventually the 'dodgy dealing' title is a thing of the past.

Contents

Introduction

Property Sourcing – The Risk Factors

It is estimated by the International Monetary Fund (IMF) that serious organised crime in the UK generates between £36 billion and £90 billion of laundered money per year. *(1)*

The purchasing of property in the UK and overseas as a means to elicit the 'cleaning' of illegally obtained monies is one of the most common methods used by criminal gangs. The advantage of using property is that a large amount of cash can be 'cleaned' in a single transaction.

Because of the immense scale of this problem and the continued hunger of criminal gangs for property, there is huge potential to damage the reputation, credibility, and livelihood of companies who are unaware of both the problem and the regulations that govern the sector.

An example of this or 'common play' by the criminal gangs is to reserve a property deal and agree to pay a 'holding deposit' or 'reservation fee' into an account (e.g. client account), they then cancel the purchase and get a refund of their cash 'cleaned' from using or abusing the system. Irrespective of the source of the money, a refund in the form of a cheque or electronic transfer from a reputable bank, company or agent, would never be questioned by the new receiving bank or institution.

Individuals or companies who do not implement adequate procedures to safeguard themselves against the risks, leave themselves wide open to exploitation by serious organised criminals who routinely source useful people whom they can exploit using criminal methods such as bribery, coercion or simply the person's ignorance of the situation and its possible consequences.

Case Study: (2)

Background - A small (one-man band) accountancy firm in South Wales with an annual turnover of £50,000. The company's clients had been met in person at their places of business, all clients were known to the owner or came on recommendation only and no new clients had been taken on for some time. Client details were entered directly into HMRC's tax system, through the accountancy office log in for future tax submission purposes.

Although the owner did not keep any written records of client details, had no written policies or procedures for dealing with new clients or the ongoing monitoring of existing clients, he believed that entering their details into HMRC's system would be sufficient for Anti-Money Laundering compliance purposes.

The company was fined £3,750 for failures in Anti-Money Laundering compliance in October 2016 (fine upheld on appeal). The fines were for the following breaches:

1. _Client Due Diligence procedures did not meet requirements._
2. _The 'ongoing monitoring' procedures did not meet requirements._
3. _The procedure for record keeping did not meet requirements._
4. _The procedures for risk assessment of clients did not meet requirements._

I think that there are two important lessons to be learned from this case: a) you are never too small for HMRC to be interested in you or find you, b) whilst this is an accountancy company and not an estate agency type business, the Money Laundering Regulations and compliance requirements are the same for everyone.

Over the past 5 ½ years of studying legislation and regulation for the property-sourcing sector, I have developed this simple 12-step process outlined below; if followed correctly, it ensures both initial and ongoing compliance within the sector.

12 STEPS FOR SUCCESSFUL PROPERTY SOURCING COMPLIANCE

STEP 1
Understand what Property Sourcing is

STEP 2
Decide on trading status e.g. Sole Trader or Ltd Company etc.

STEP 3
Study and get a good understanding of relevant legislation and regulation

STEP 4
Obtain Professional Indemnity plus other relevant Insurance

STEP 5
Register with one of three Government Approved Property Redress Schemes

STEP 6
Register for Data Protection

STEP 7
Register for Anti-Money Laundering

STEP 8
Understand the Due Diligence Processes

STEP 9
Create your Legal Contracts and Terms of Business

STEP 10
Create your Policies and Procedures

STEP 11
Understand on going compliance (training)

STEP 12
Keep up to date with changes

I hope that you find my book engaging and practical; this is your journey so let's make it a great one!

Chapter 1 – What is Property Sourcing?

So, you are an investor and buy property deals from property sourcers, or you are a property sourcer who sources deals, packages them and sells them on for a fee … how can this book help YOU?

<u>Property Sourcers</u> – After reading this book, you will have the knowledge required to set up a new, compliant property sourcing business or if you are already 'up and running', adapt your existing business in area(s) that you may not have been aware of or were unsure about.

However, if you choose to ignore the guidance contained in this book, then you risk being on the receiving end of fines up to £15,000 just for failing to register with compulsory regulators or unlimited fines and a possible 14 years prison sentence (1) for serious breaches of the regulations, which govern it.

<u>Investors</u> – As an investor, you will have a much greater understanding as to what questions you need to ask a property sourcer, what checks you can make to ensure that they are working in compliance with ALL legislation and regulation with regard to the property sector.

However, if you choose to ignore the guidance contained in this book, then you put yourself at risk of being on the receiving end of unscrupulous 'deal packagers' who have only their best interests at heart and potentially lose YOU tens of thousands of pounds in the process with no easy route for recourse!

I have written this book so that you can either read the whole thing, make notes and soak up the necessary knowledge, or use it as a pocket guide dipping in and out as you need or, take one chapter at a time working your way through from beginning to end, by which time you should have a very good understanding of what compliance with the regulations and legislation that govern our industry looks like.

For ease of use, at the end of pertinent chapters, I have created a section called 'Key Points to Take Away', these highlight facts that would be pertinent to either an Investor or Property Sourcer. This works to emphasise what you have learned within that chapter but also acts as a quick reference point to refer back to should your memory need refreshing in the future.

I have always found this book style to be useful not just for a single read but also as an ongoing reference book; I hope that you find this works for you too.

Whilst this book is certainly not about how to source property investment deals, I think it is important that you have at least a basic understanding of what property sourcing actually is. To me, property sourcing is the finding of property related investment opportunities that provide a 'win, win, win' situation for the investor, seller, and sourcer. It is vital that any sourcing agent bring their knowledge of the area, investment types, and negotiation skills together to ensure that they acquire the best deals possible for their clients. I also firmly believe that no property deal acquired should leave the seller in a worse financial state than you found them in. Why you might ask? Well, because the property sector fundamentally is not about bricks and mortar – it's about people, and those people have husbands, wives, sons, and daughters whose lives could be seriously affected by your attitude as to how you source those investment deals.

When you stop and think about it, to obtain a property or site that offers a good financial return for the investor, the seller must be at least to some degree, in a distressed state. In general, the level of the distress will directly relate to the level of discount on purchase price that you might hope to achieve. For example, a seller that has no mortgage on a property and is merely testing the market to see how much they might get is certainly not distressed; however, a seller who is in debt, divorcing or moving areas for work could be highly motivated to sell the property or site at a greater discounted purchase price.

At the earliest stage of my relationship with a seller, I always make it clear that I will only work with them if doing so leaves them no worse off financially than they already are. We would say something like "... We will be completely honest with you if we feel that we cannot help you or if by trying to help you our actions would potentially make your situation worse..." In that case, we would signpost them to other sources of help such as an independent financial advisor or possibly Citizens Advice, etc.

Deal sourcing is not just about the money gained in fees; I believe it is mainly about the people involved and the experience that they have from working with you. Below is an example of one of our own 'direct to vendor' potential deals that just would not work:

Early on in our property-sourcing journey, we received a lead from one of our leaflet campaigns, sadly we could not help because of the following:

- *The potential client needed full or even above market value for their property, as they needed to buy a bungalow due to declining health.*

- *Although they had little or no mortgage on the property, they were not interested in re-mortgaging with a BTL mortgage, renting the property out and using the cash released to buy a bungalow.*

- *They were prepared to wait for an acceptable offer.*

- *To try to push them into 'doing a deal' with us would not only have stressed them and possibly made health issues worse but also create debt in the form of a new mortgage should they rent out their home at a time when health issues were becoming a serious concern for them.*

After many months, they did eventually sell and buy the bungalow that they had long dreamed of.

Who are Agents?

An estate agent works in the way that we are all used to when selling our own homes. They work with the seller, and their fees are based on getting the highest price possible for them:

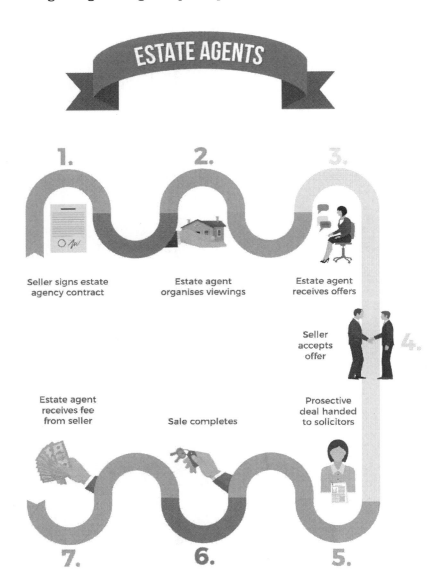

In complete contrast to the estate agent, a sourcing agent usually works with the investor or buyer, seeking to achieve the lowest purchase price possible:

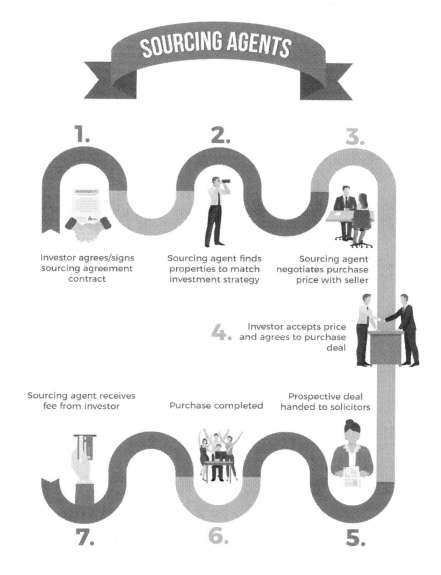

The sourcing agent searches for property deals that have a benefit for the investor:

- Significant discount on purchase price
- Ability to add value through refurbishment or extension
- Convert to another use producing improved cash-flow

As a sourcer, you may be thinking that you could take a fee from both the seller and the investor for a deal and make even more money; I should point out that it may well be considered unethical for an agent to receive a fee from both the seller and the investor in relation to the same deal; this is because the agent could not best represent the interests of both parties at the same time, the seller wanting the highest price possible, and the investor wanting the lowest price possible.

So, for all of those who believe that sourcing agents are not estate agents and, therefore, the legislation and regulations have no bearing at all on what they do:

Definition of an Estate Agent:

For the purposes of section 1 of the Estate Agency Act 1979, estate agency work includes introducing and/or negotiating with people who want to buy or sell freehold or leasehold property (or their Scottish equivalents) including commercial or agricultural property where this is done:

*In the course of a business 'and' *Pursuant to instructions from a client

In plain simple terms, what does that mean? Well, basically that means that even if you have only a verbal agreement with an investor to source a property or site for them, you only introduce them to a seller and in return for that service you receive a fee, then you are governed by the Estate Agency Act 1979 and all of the other regulations and legislation that cover this sector.

Property sourcing when done legally, compliant, and ethically, can provide a lucrative source of income. If you are completely new to the property investment sector, have little or no cash with which to invest yourself, don't worry as many before you have used sourcing as a route firstly to build up a larger 'cash pot' but also along the way gained valuable knowledge and developed invaluable long-term relationships with experienced investors.

It is my opinion these relationships are vital to your long-term success, as a large number of 'High Net Worth' investors have vast experience in various niche investment sectors such as Houses of Multiple Occupation (HMO's), Serviced Accommodation (SA), Rent to Rent (R2R) as well as the commercial and residential development sectors. The relationships that you develop with them over a period of time create the well known 'know, like, trust' scenario which could lead to opportunities for you to work with them, allowing you to move up to much larger projects providing larger financial returns.

Why would these investors work with you? Imagine how happy they would be if you secured them an investment deal that would net them £100,000 in profit or a buy to let property that gave them a 10%+ yield. Do you think they would be happy to pay you a fee of £3,000, £5,000, or even £10,000+ in exchange for a great return? Of course they would. For most people, you wouldn't need many deals to complete in a year to make a big difference to your current income, or even give up your day job and work in property full time.

When you are looking for great investment deals for yourself, you are almost certain to come across great deals that just don't fit in with your strategy but would absolutely work for someone else. There is nothing wrong with packaging up that deal and selling to another investor as long as it is done legally and ethically.

Just like any other sector, there are positive gains to be had as well as pain should you fail to comply with relevant legislation & regulation.

As far as sourcing agents are concerned, the penalties are as follows:

- Failure to register with compulsory bodies – Up to £15,000 fine
- Failure to comply with regulations and standards – Up to 14 years imprisonment, unlimited fine and unlimited civil penalties

The property sector is considered to be at serious risk of abuse from money laundering, terrorist gangs and agents failing to comply with regulations whilst at the same time making lots of money misleading both sellers and investors.

The professional bodies for our sector are watching; could you afford a £15,000 fine?

Key points to take away

Sourcing Agents:

1. Property Sourcing is a great way to gain knowledge of the property investment sector even if you do not have a cash pot of your own to invest initially.

2. The property sector is a 'people' business and not just 'bricks and mortar'.

3. There are regulations and legislation that MUST be followed.

4. Failure to follow the rules could lead to a heavy fine or even imprisonment.

Investors:

1. If you are cash rich and time poor then using the services of a professional sourcer makes sense.

2. Be aware that not all property sources are made equal, some are ignorant of the regulations, some simply ignore the regulations and some don't give a damn about you or your hard earned cash.

3. Could you afford to lose several thousand pounds, or more? Make sure that you know who you are working with.

4. Stay up to date with changes that may affect how you work with your chosen sourcer or for your own protection should anything go wrong.

Chapter 2 – How to avoid a heavy fine or even a stretch behind bars

So, what do you need to understand to avoid that heavy fine or spending time behind bars? Well, a good start would be to have at least a basic understanding of the legislation and regulation that governs the property sector.

Firstly, what is the difference between them? In simple terms, Legislation (L) are laws passed by Parliament and Regulations (R) are written, usually by the professional body that governs the relevant sector, to assist in the enforcement of that law.

Below is a glimpse at the legislation and regulation for the property sourcing sector, each providing you with a brief description or definition, outlining any expectations or penalties and also naming the relevant governing bodies linked to each. There are also links in the 'resource' section of this book to relevant and useful guides where appropriate and available.

The Estate Agents Act 1979 (L)

This act applies to persons carrying out 'estate agency work' as described in section 1. (See Chapter 1 for a detailed description). It was implemented to ensure that estate agents run their businesses in the best interests of their clients and that both buyers and sellers are treated honestly, fairly, and promptly.

You do not have to describe yourself as an estate agent; if you are a broker or a lead generator and source a deal i.e. introduce a seller to potential buyers or vice versa and then take any steps to achieve a sale, you are governed by the Act and liable to penalties for failure to comply.

What is expected of you?

☐ You must provide clients with specific information in writing with regard to your fees and charges for services before agreeing to act for them.

☐ Disclose to a client any services you are offering/intend to offer to a prospective buyer/seller or any financial benefit that you may gain from the acceptance of those services by the buyer/seller.

☐ You must disclose any personal interest that you, the company or any other employee of your company have, in relation to any sale.

☐ Promptly inform clients in writing of any offers received and the financial status of any prospective buyer.

☐ Handle clients' money professionally.

☐ Be a member of an officially approved estate agents redress scheme.

Governing Body: The National Trading Standards Estate Agency Team (NTSEAT) currently Powys County Council (PCC) the 'lead enforcement authority' for the Estate Agents Act 1979 with support from Isle of Anglesey Council (IoAC).

What are the penalties for failure to comply?

1. Warnings if found to be in breach of any part of the Act.

2. Various governing bodies can apply to the court for a 'Prohibition Order' to ban the company or individual from operating as an estate agency type business.

3. To ignore a prohibition order is a criminal offence, which could lead to a fine.

The Consumers, Estate Agents and Redress Act 2007 (CEARA) (L)

This Act made it a requirement for ALL estate agency type businesses, in the United Kingdom, to belong to a recognised, independent redress scheme (alternatively known as an Ombudsman) since 1st October 2008. It also implemented measures aimed at improving the way that estate agency type businesses work.

What is expected of you?

☐ Register with one of the three government approved schemes.

☐ Comply with the scheme's 'code of conduct'.

☐ Abide by the Ombudsman's decisions with regard to a formal complaint.

☐ Requires agents to make and keep records, including: offer letters for 6 years.

Governing Body: NTSEAT & Local Trading Standards

What are the penalties for failure to comply?

1. Warnings if found to be in breach of any part of the Act.

2. Various governing bodies can apply to the court for a 'Prohibition Order' to ban the company or individual from operating as an estate agency type business.

3. To ignore a prohibition order is a criminal offence, which could lead to a fine.

The Data Protection Act 1998 (L)

This act regulates the use and storage of 'personal data', which is defined as any data, which relates to a living individual who can be identified:

a) From that data or,

b) From data and other information which is in the possession of, or is likely to come into the possession of, the data controller (a person who determines the purpose for which personal data is processed), and includes any expression of opinion about the individual and any indication of the intentions of the data controller or any other person in respect of the individual.

The data can be held in paper format, storage devices or cloud-based. This includes data collected from automated response systems such as Aweber or Mailchimp for example:

a) Your company receives a request from your website contact page or other online source to receive update emails, the information provided by that person asking for the updates e.g. name and email address are classified as personal data.

b) Your company holds data, which is cloud-based within a CRM system. These records do not include names but have a unique reference number, which can be matched back to paper documents to identify the client. The information held in the cloud is classed as personal data.

There are strict rules to follow, which are known as, 'data protection principles'.

What is expected of you?

☐ <u>Fair and Lawful</u> – Have legitimate grounds for collecting and using personal data, do not use data in such a way as to cause unjustified adverse effects on the individual, be transparent about how you intend to use the data (privacy notices, etc.) Handle personal date only in ways that would be expected and ensure that you do not do anything unlawful with the data.

☐ Purposes – Ensure that you are open about your reasons for collecting data, comply with the Act's fair processing requirements, notifying the Information Commissioner and ensure that if you wish to use or disclose personal data for reasons other than originally stated at time of collection, the new use or disclosure is fair.

☐ Adequacy – The data held should be sufficient for the purpose you are holding it for in relation to that person, and you do not hold more information than is needed for that purpose.

☐ Accuracy – You must take reasonable steps to ensure the accuracy of the data being held, ensure that the source of the data is clear, consider any challenges to the accuracy of the information and consider when it may be necessary to update the information.

☐ Retention – There are no specific maximum or minimum periods for retaining data within the Act. The Act does say that personal data should not be kept any longer than is necessary for the purpose or purposes that it was obtained. Carry out regularly reviews of the data that you hold, consider whether you still require the data, update, archive or if no longer required securely delete the information.

☐ Rights – The individual whose personal data you hold has a right of access to a copy of information held. A right to object to processing if it is likely to cause damage or stress. A right to prevent processing for direct marketing. A right in certain circumstances to have inaccurate data rectified, blocked, erased or destroyed and a right to claim compensation for damages caused by a breach of the Act.

- ☐ <u>Security</u> – You must have appropriate security measures to prevent personal data that you hold from being accidentally or deliberately compromised. You must use security that is designed for the level of personal data that you hold. Be clear about who in your company is responsible for ensuring that information is secure. Make sure that you have the correct physical and technical security in place, backed by robust policies and procedures with reliable, well-trained staff and are ready to respond to any breach in security swiftly and effectively.

- ☐ <u>International</u> – If considering sending personal data outside the European Economic Area, (EEA) then there is a 10-point checklist within the ICO guide to help you understand what is required.

In 2016, the ICO issued 21 fines totalling £2,155,500, in January 2017 issued 2 fines totalling £170,000(1)

The European Union's General Data Protection Regulations (GDPR) were finalised in April 2016 and will come into effect from May 2018. Whether the UK stays in Europe or not, we will have to adopt equivalent regulations for ourselves, so it would be wise for companies to be aware of the changes and adapt accordingly as leaving it to the last minute could prove to be very expensive as *penalties will rise from the current maximum of £500,000 up to a maximum of 4% of annual turnover or €20million, whichever is the greater.

As well as all compliance for the above, by May 2018 your company will be required to be able to provide upon request the following:

- ☐ Explicit consent for use of data collected

- ☐ Must 'Opt In' rather than 'Opt Out' of a call to action or request for a person to make contact and provide personal contact details, such as email or telephone number

- The right to request that data be deleted/destroyed

- Mandatory reporting for serious breaches to ICO within 72 hours of breach – Any breach that may cause personal data to be accessed

- Must have policy and procedure in place to deal with a suspected breach

You must be able to prove that you obtained consent to market to and for what purpose. For example, if someone signs up to receive a four weekly newsletter from you, then that is all that you can send to them. You cannot send other information or current deals available unless the person actively 'opted in' to receive all of those things at the time of signing up. You must be able to demonstrate valid consent and record how and when that consent was given.

How could you achieve this?

- Ensure that your 'Consent Statement' is clear and easily visible

- Include a link to your complaint, privacy, and cookie policies

- Make sure that you keep an audit trail, a record of what was signed up for including time and date

- There MUST be a clear path to 'opt out' on every email

- You MUST get your current database or CRM correctly opted in!

Any information that you currently hold on clients, potential clients, leads or simple contacts will need to be reviewed for current accuracy and how that information was gathered. The proof that you have, will it be sufficient to comply with the new regulations?

It is hoped that these 'tightening' up of the regulations will create better quality data being held, which will lead to better business and ultimately much less spam.

Governing Body: Information Commissioners Office (ICO).

---

*What are the penalties for failure to comply or register?

1. For failure to register: Maximum fine at Magistrates Court is £5,000, maximum fine at Crown Court is unlimited.

2. For minor breaches: Commit to taking course of action to improve or receive an enforcement notice

3. For serious breaches: Maximum fine of up to £500,000

4. For deliberate breaches: Possible prison sentences

UK Anti-Money Laundering Legislation (AMLL)

The Proceeds of Crime Act 2002 (PoCA) (L) (as amended by the Crime and Courts Act 2013 and the Serious Crime Act 2015).

This Act and its amendments created a number of money laundering offences. The key activity relevant to property sourcing would be 'the buying and selling of real property (land or buildings) or business entities.'

What is expected of you?

☐ You must be aware of where your investor's funds originated from e.g. property sale, retirement or bereavement and have proof of this.

☐ Your due diligence process is crucial to compliance. (See Chapter 6)

What are the penalties for failure to comply?

1. The principle Money Laundering offences carry a maximum penalty up to 14 years imprisonment and/or unlimited fine.

Terrorism Act 2000 (TA) (L) (as amended by the Anti-Terrorism, Crime and Security Act 2001, The Terrorism Act 2006 and the Terrorism Act 2000 and Proceeds of Crime Act (Amendment) Regulations 2007

Definition

"Fundraising, possessing or dealing with property or facilitating someone else to do so, when intending, knowing or suspecting or having reasonable cause to suspect that it is intended for purposes of terrorism."

What is expected of you?

☐ Be aware that money or property could be used for the purposes of terrorism.

☐ Purchase funds could have been obtained from the commission of acts of terrorism

☐ Profits from a project may be used for the purposes of terrorism.

☐ It is an offence to be involved in fundraising if you have knowledge or reasonable cause to believe that money or other property may be used for terrorist purposes

As a property sourcer, should a terrorist organisation use you to source property investments where the purchase money and/or any subsequent profits are for the purposes of carrying on terrorist activity, then you may be in breach of this Act.

Financing for the provision of terrorism could be the handling of cash (reservation fees or deposits) or the purchasing/selling of property, either could be legitimately sourced or from criminal activities and involve large or small quantities of money.

Governing Body: HMRC

What are the penalties for failure to comply?

1. The principle Money Laundering offences carry a maximum penalty up to 14 years imprisonment and/or unlimited fine.

Money Laundering Regulations 2007 (updated 2012) (MLR) (R)

Definition

'To acquire, possess or deal in a benefit obtained from a criminal act or to facilitate someone else to do so, when knowing or suspecting that the benefit was obtained from a criminal act.'

The regulations require that anyone working within a regulated sector get to know and monitor their clients and the services provided to them. They impose duties upon sole traders and companies (not employees) to establish and maintain policies and procedures to detect and deter activities relating to money laundering and terrorist financing.

What is expected of you?

Both PoCA & TA define money laundering and terrorist financing and impose very similar obligations on those regulated by the sector. There is no industry standard, and so the following list is a brief overview of the actions that an agent should complete to achieve basic compliance:

- Decide who will be the 'Nominated Officer' and senior responsible person known as the Money Laundering Reporting Officer (MLRO). The overall person responsible for overseeing money-laundering compliance must be high-level management dependent on the size and structure of your company; for example, if you have a board of directors, then one of those directors must be nominated as the overall responsible person.

- Decide whether to apply Money Laundering (ML) Procedures across all services (N.B.: it is dangerous to make any service or staff member 'Zero' rated for ML compliance).

- The nominated person should familiarise themselves with the Money Laundering Regulations.

- Identify both 'Low' and 'High' risk activities carried out by your company.

- Implement procedures that specify the steps to be taken when verifying a client's identification, using a 'Risk Sensitive' approach.

- Implementing procedures for the scrutinising of receipts and payments.

- Submit Internal Suspicion Reports to a MLRO.

- Submit a Suspicious Activity Report (SAR) to the Serious Organised Crime Agency (SOCA).

- Must carry out a simple risk assessment process to assess risks posed by your clients.

With the implementation of the 4th Money Laundering Directive in Summer 2017 the following actions are also be required:

☐ All estate agents, even if their fees are payable by the seller, will have to carry out due diligence on the buyer, taking into account their responsibilities under the money laundering regulations. I expect that as far as property sourcers are concerned that although their contracts are with the buyer that they should also carry out checks on the seller if they do not already do so as part of their due diligence process.

☐ You must carry out audits on money laundering policies and procedures, although it is not stated who should carry out these audits or how frequently but thought that an annual audit by a person at director level would be acceptable.

☐ All estate agency type businesses carry out a Disclosure and Barring Service (DBS) check on their staff, although not as yet clear as to whether that will be all staff or just customer facing. (We are waiting for guidance to be released on this).

Governing Body: HMRC

What are the penalties for failure to comply or register?

1. Failure to register up to unlimited fine and/or up to two years imprisonment

2. The principle Money Laundering offences carry a maximum penalty for breaches of up to 14 years imprisonment and or unlimited fine.

The Bribery Act 2010 (L)

This Act came into effect on 1st July 2011 and made it a criminal

44

offence for commercial organisations including partnerships, which fail to prevent bribery by anyone working on behalf of a business that intends to obtain or retain business or business advantage as a result of the bribe.

Definition

A bribe is a: *'financial or other advantage' offered, promised or given to another person with the intention of inducing them to 'perform improperly' a function or activity in the course of their business or employment, or of rewarding them having done so.'*

The phrase 'financial or other advantage' includes not just money or other obvious benefit types such as gifts and entertainment, but also preferential treatment in any context.

The phrase 'perform improperly' is most simply understood as a person not carrying out their profession or employment in the way that should be expected of them, their employees or those responsible for their employment.

When liaising with other estate agents, letting agents or sourcers who provide you with property leads, you may end up working with only one particular person within that company, but if you give a gift just to that individual, purchased just for them and not for the office as a whole, then that could be perceived as a 'bribe', an enticement for them to continue to provide deals just to you.

You must also consider the value of any gift given in relation to the value of the service that had been provided. For example, an agent sends you a property deal, which leads to a £3,000 sourcing fee, so as a thank you, you buy them a three-day trip to New York costing £2,000. I think you would agree, in this case, the value of the gift given is excessive in comparison to the value of the original service. Perhaps a moderately priced bottle of wine would have been more appropriate.

What is expected of you?

There are six principles to follow in deciding the level of policies and procedures that your company might need to implement:

☐ Proportionality: Action taken should be proportionate to the risk posed, e.g. a small company operating in markets where bribery is not prevalent against a larger company working in overseas or sectors where bribery may be widespread.

☐ Top Level Commitment: Those people at the 'top' (Directors) need to show that they make sure that ALL staff are aware of the company's bribery procedures and will not tolerate such behaviour within their workplace.

☐ Risk Assessment: Carry out research into the markets that you operate in and the types of people that you deal with. Use this information to carry out a risk assessment and develop company procedures to mitigate any risk.

☐ Due Diligence: Know your client and your staff.

☐ Communication: It is essential that those at the 'top' (Directors) effectively communicate the companies' policies and procedures to ALL staff members. Additional training may be required for those staff that are supplier or customer facing.

☐ Monitoring and Review: With an increase in the size of your business, the number of staff employed or a change to the sector that you work in may alter the day-to-day risks that you face. Ongoing monitoring of your bribery policies and procedures are therefore essential.

Governing Body: HMRC

What are the penalties for failure to comply?

1. Maximum fine of up to £10,000 in England & Wales

2. Up to 10 years in prison.

The Consumers Contracts (Information, Cancellation and Additional Charges) Regulations 2013 (R)

These regulations replaced the Consumer Protection (Distance Selling) Regulations 2000, often referred to as the Distance Selling Regulations. It also replaced the Cancellation of Contracts made in a Consumer's Home or Place of Work Regulations 2008. They cover the use of contracts both on and off business premises.

From a property sourcing perspective, this regulation could relate to contracts with both sellers and buyers.

What is expected of you?

There is a requirement to provide detailed information to your client:

□   The main details of the services provided

□   Your identity – such as trading name

□   The geographical address where you are established, including a telephone number and email to allow easy and quick communication for the consumer.

□   If acting on behalf of another trader, their identity and geographical address.

□   If the address for consumer complaints is different to your geographical address, this must be given.

- Total cost of services provided, inclusive of VAT, or how this will be calculated.

- Details of any other costs incurable.

- The monthly, or billing period costs of open-ended contracts or subscriptions.

- Your complaint handling policy.

- The conditions, time limits, and procedure for exercising a right to cancel.

- For service contracts, a consumer can ask you to start providing the service within the cancellation period; you must tell them that they will be required to pay you reasonable costs for any services provided up to the time of cancellation (14 days, starting the day after the day on which the contract is made).

- If you are a member of a 'code of conduct', you must inform consumers how they can obtain a copy of the code (providing a link to the appropriate section of the code sponsors' website).

- Inform of any requirement to give deposits or reservation fees, etc.

Governing body: Trading Standards Office

What are the penalties for failure to comply?

1. Consumers could prosecute for breach of contract.

2. Trading Standards could apply to court for an order requiring you to comply.

3. If you fail to comply with the court order, the maximum penalty is a fine and up to two years imprisonment.

The Consumer Protection from Unfair Trading Regulations (October 2008) (CPR's) (R)

The CPR's replaced the Property Misdescriptions Act 1991 and prohibits you and your business from carrying out unfair commercial practices when dealing with clients across all sectors of business. These include but are not limited to, unfair or misleading trading practices, misleading omissions, and aggressive sales tactics.

The regulations introduce the terms:

'Average Consumer', 'Material Information' and
'Transactional Decision'.

Average Consumer – Someone who is reasonably informed, observant, and circumspect. Would pay some attention to documents although not necessarily the small print, unless pointed out to them, and would probably check out publically available facts for themselves if simple to do so.

Material Information – Any information provided or omitted that could cause the consumer to make a transactional decision that they would not have taken otherwise.

Transactional Decision – This is a step that is taken to progress towards an end goal, for instance, when you want to buy a property, the first step that you take is probably to view several properties to make an informed choice, the viewing of a property is considered to be a 'Transactional Decision'. Although other examples could be, make an offer, carry out a survey, instruct a solicitor, or apply for a mortgage, etc.

These regulations only cover the sale of property to consumers

49

(private individuals). For the sale of commercial property, similar provisions exist in the Marketing Business Protection from Misleading Regulations 2008 (BPR's).

What is expected of you?

Treat your clients fairly:

☐ Do not make false or misleading statements that would cause your client to do something that if they had all of the facts or the truth they would not have done

☐ Do not use aggressive practices or exert undue pressure

☐ Do not engage in banned practices – For example, claim to be a member of a professional body when you are not

☐ Do not fail to show professionalism in all aspects of your service – For example, part-time staff members advising inappropriately as their training was poor or inappropriate

In short, when assessing a potential property deal, ensure that you gather all relevant information, ask pertinent questions, think about what situations may cause a purchase to fall through; such as short property lease, serious flooding issues, severe neighbour dispute, etc. Possibly ask something along the lines of:

"... Is there anything that you can think of that a buyer would want to know"?

Record what questions and answers were asked and any responses; record any enquiries that you make and always the reasons why you decided not to disclose a piece of information.

You are obliged to seek out information you need to obtain and retain information, ensuring that your marketing material is accurate and balanced.

Ask yourself, if you were the buyer, what would you want to know?

> Governing Body: Local Trading Standards or
> Advertising Standards Authority

What are the penalties for failure to comply?

1. Cases heard in the Magistrates Court: Maximum fine of £5,000 per offence.

2. Cases heard in the Crown Court: Unlimited fine and/or up to two years Imprisonment.

The Business Protection from Misleading Marketing Regulations (October 2008) (BPR's) (R)

These regulations replaced The Control of Misleading Advertisements Regulations 1988 (CMAR's) and prohibit traders from all sectors including estate agents from using misleading practices in any business to business advertisements or misleading marketing used when advertising a property for sale.

What is an advertisement: Any form of representation made in connection with your business in order to supply or transfer a product, goods, services or immovable property.

What could be Misleading: If the advertisement deceives or is likely to deceive and that deception is likely to affect the economic behaviour of or cause financial loss to that trader.

What is expected of you?

☐ Do not use misleading practices or advertisements

You can use in your defence any evidence recorded that you took all reasonable steps in your due diligence process when obtaining the information that you used in your advertisement.

> Governing Body: Local Trading Standards or
> Advertising Standards Authority

What are the penalties for failure to comply?

1. Cases heard in the Magistrates Court: Maximum fine of £5,000 per offence.

2. Cases heard in the Crown Court: Unlimited fine and/or up to 2 years Imprisonment.

Consumer Rights Act 2015 (L)

This act came into force on 1st October 2015 and replaced the Sale of Goods Act 1979 and the Supply of Goods and Services Act 1982. It outlines a consumer's route if they feel that the goods or services provided failed to do what was promised, it also clarifies the terms and conditions that are considered to be unfair.

What is expected of you?

☐ If you use digital content to advertise your service (estate agency work is included in the act) or provide digital downloads (paid for, or supplied free with other products paid for) to your consumers, you must provide your terms of service for your products, making it clear what the consumer should do if they are not happy with their purchase (reports or courses, etc.).

☐ Your contracts and terms of business should be fair, no hidden fees or charges, for example.

This is also the legislation that made it compulsory for ALL letting agents to publicise all of their fees.

Governing Body: Local Trading Standards Officer

What are the penalties for failure to comply?

Known as 'Enhanced Consumer Measures' (EMC's):

1. To reimburse the customer for financial loss suffered as a result of a breach of consumer law.

2. To pay a sum to a consumer charity.

3. To advertise the breach in the press, on their website and in place(s) of business, and

4. To overhaul the internal practices to avoid a repeat of the breach.

Electronic Commerce (EC Directive) Regulations 2002 (R)

These regulations incorporate the EU Electronic Commerce Directive 2000 and apply to businesses that sell goods or services to businesses or consumers via the internet; virtually every commercial website is covered by these regulations, email or SMS text messages where contracts are concluded by electronic means over distance; for example, advertise a property deal on the internet and conclude a deal remotely with a buyer.

What is expected of you?

These regulations state specific information that your business

MUST provide to recipients of online services, also providing guidance for advertising and promotions. If you provide information services via a website, you must provide the following information to recipients, to create trust and confidence in the service provided:

- ☐ The name of the service provider

- ☐ The service provider's established geographical address (does not have to be the legal address)

- ☐ Service provider contact details, including email, to which contact can be quickly made

- ☐ If the service provider is registered to a trade (such as NAEA or ARLA) or other professional registration (such as a solicitor or accountant), provide details

- ☐ Company registration number or other means of identification

- ☐ If you provide a contract online, your customer should be able to print and store a copy of the terms and conditions

- ☐ Must be clear about all steps required to conclude the contract, for example, 'Click Here'.

- ☐ Make clear whether you will be storing the completed contract and if accessible

- ☐ What relevant codes of conduct you follow and provide links to them
- ☐ Your website MUST allow customers to go back and correct mistakes made during the order process before the order is placed.

- Once order placed, you must acknowledge receipt without undue delay

---

Governing Body: Trading Standards Office

What are the penalties for failure to comply?

1. Consumer may take out private prosecution for damages.

2. Local Trading Standards Officer or other named consumer-protection body may apply to court for an enforcement order, known as a 'Stop Now' order for breaches of the regulation.

3. Failure to comply with the court order would be considered to be contempt of court, punishable by fines and/or imprisonment.

Enterprise Act 2002 (L)

This act was created to provide a framework for enforcement officers to protect consumers where there has been an act or omission in the course of business, where a company misleads clients or generally behaves in an unfair manner, which is harmful to the 'Collective interests of Consumers in the UK'.

What is expected of you?

- Treat your clients fairly.

- Do not mislead your clients.

Governing Body: Trading Standards Officers

What are the penalties for failure to comply?

1. Trading Standards Officers can apply to court for an enforcement order preventing a company from repeating the offence.

Provision of Services Regulations 2009 (R)

Introduced to govern businesses that supply services in the UK, covering estate agency type businesses. The information below can be available on the website or provided as part of the contractual documentation process.

What is expected of you?

The following information must be made available:

☐ Where a complaint or a request for more information can be sent

☐ The service providers: Name, address, legal status and VAT number

☐ Details of any trade registrations or other membership schemes

☐ The main features of any 'after sales' guarantees offered

☐ Details of Public Liability Insurance (service provider required to hold)

☐ Details of dispute resolution procedure (from code of conduct of any professional registered body linked to)

Governing Body: Local Trading Standards

What are the penalties for failure to comply?

1. Consumers must seek recompense through the court via a private prosecution.

Financial Services and Markets Act 2000 (FSMA) (L)

Financial promotions are regulated through the Financial Services and Markets Act 2000; Section 21 of the legislation highlights restrictions for financial promotions:

Definition of a 'Financial Promotion':

'An invitation or inducement to engage in investment activity, communicated by a person in the course of business'.

What is expected of you?

☐ All promotions must be clear, fair, and not misleading.

☐ All promotions must be balanced and provide accurate information.

Governing Body: Financial Conduct Authority (FCA)

What are the penalties for failure to comply?

1. You can be required to immediately withdraw or amend a misleading promotion.

2. Liable for a fine

3. Up to two years imprisonment

Performance of Buildings (England and Wales) Regulations 2012 (R)

These regulations state that it is the responsibility of the seller to provide an energy performance certificate (EPC) to any potential buyer. If the property is rented, then it is the responsibility of the landlord to provide an EPC to any potential tenant. An agent for either the landlord or the seller is responsible to ensure that an EPC has at least been commissioned prior to marketing and all efforts must be made to ensure that an EPC has been obtained within seven days of first marketing the property.

It is worth noting that if your property deal is a self-contained apartment/flat, each apartment/flat MUST have its own EPC certificate, not the building as a whole.

This regulation states that you must have a current EPC certificate when constructing, selling or renting a property. It shows the energy efficiency rating of the building and is valid for 10 years.

The EPC is only valid when it is registered with one of the two Energy Performance Registers (EPC Register):

☐ The Domestic Energy Performance Certificate Register – EPC's for dwellings

☐ The Non-Domestic Energy Performance Register – For non-domestic and public buildings

What is expected of you?

☐ Ensure that before you market a property for sale that the seller has at least commissioned a report and that a copy will be available within the first seven days of your marketing commencing.

- Details of the energy rating MUST be included in sales marketing particulars.

> Governing Body: Trading Standards Authority

What are the penalties for failure to comply?

- From April 2014, the penalty for failure to display the energy rating of the property in marketing material for either sale or rental is £200 per advertisement/property.

As property sourcers, we often deal directly with a vendor, so you must be aware of the fact that prior to selling their property, the vendor MUST have at least applied for an EPC certificate prior to marketing and all efforts must be made to ensure that an EPC has been obtained within seven days of first marketing the property.

The Town and Country Planning (Control of Advertisements) Regulations 2007 (R)

These regulations cover the use of agency 'For Sale', 'Sold' or 'To Let' boards outside properties, giving 'deemed planning consent' as long as maximum size requirements are met. The regulations state that once a property has been 'Let' or 'Sold', the sign must be removed after 14 days.

What is expected of you?

- If as an agent you use advertising boards to indicate a property for sale or to let, once the property is 'sold' or 'let', the sign should be removed from outside the property within 14 days of the completion of sale or the agreement of a tenancy.

> Governing Body: Local Planning Authorities

What are the penalties for failure to comply?

☐ There is a maximum fine of £2,500 for breaches with an ongoing daily fine of £250 for continuation of breaches after conviction.

Estate Agents (Accounts) Regulations 1981 (R)

These regulations set down how clients' money (contract and pre-contract deposits*) are held and recorded. A contract deposit is any sum, which forms part (or whole) of the purchase for a deal and is paid on or after the exchange of contracts. Pre-contract deposits are any amount of money paid, for example, as a reservation fee, prior to the exchange of an enforceable contract.

Authorised institutions:

☐ The Bank of England
☐ Recognised bank or other licensed institution (as per: Banking Act 1979)
☐ The Post Office
☐ Trustees Savings Bank
☐ Designated Building Society

When operating a client account, you should always instruct your bank, or other institution, that the money is to be held separately from the company's own money. Bank charges for operating all client accounts must be paid from other resources and not charged against the account.

What is expected of you?

☐ Anyone carrying out estate agency type work must hold any client monies received in a separate client account, the account must be in the name of the estate agency and have the term 'Client' in the title.

- The agent is accountable for interest on any deposits held in the account unless the agent is a 'Stakeholder' or the deposit is less than £500 or the interest payable is less than £10. If the account holds multiple deposits, then the client would be entitled to an appropriate portion of any interest earned. If the deposit is NOT paid into an appropriate client account, then the client is entitled to an interest payment requisite to which could have been earned in the highest rated interest account with the institution used by the agent.

- Permitted transactions:

  - Contract or pre-contract deposits
  - Minimum sum required to open or maintaining the account
  - Any sum required to rectify an error in paying monies out of the account (in contravention of the regulations)

- Permitted payments out of the account:

  - Payment to the client entitled to monies
  - Remuneration for estate agency work (with clients agreement)
  - To exercise a lien (1) which the agent is entitled to
  - To transfer to another client account
  - To withdraw monies incorrectly paid to that account
  - Where non-client monies were required to open or maintain an account

It is therefore logical that a compliant client account should NEVER be overdrawn.

- Client account records MUST include:

a) General

- Title of the client account into which money is paid
- Date of payment
- Name of institution (Bank) the account is held with

b) Receipts

- The amount
- Name and address of payer
- Whether sum is 'contract' or 'pre-contract' monies
- Whether it includes any sum in respect of a connected contract
- Whether it includes any non-client money, and if so, for what purpose and what form was it received, e.g. cash
- The 'deal' to which the money relates
- Seller name
- Capacity in which the money was received
- Identity of the person for whom the money is being held
- Date of receipt

This information MUST be included on ALL receipts issued by the agent.

c) Payments

- The amount
- Identity of payee
- Date of payment
- Deal to which the payment relates
- Occasion on which the payment is made, e.g. refund, transfer to solicitor, etc.

All records must be kept for a period of six years after the end of the accounting period.

d) Audits

- ☐ Accounts must be audited annually by an independent accountant

- ☐ An audit trail of ALL transactions must be held for inspection

You must not hold a deposit, or any other money belonging to a client (buyer or seller) unless you are covered by adequate insurance (see Chapter 6).

Governing Body: Your Professional Body
e.g. Property Ombudsman, NAEA or RIC's

What are the penalties for failure to comply?

1. Possible expulsion from membership of the professional body

Companies Act 2006, and the Companies, Limited Liability Partnership and Business (Names and Trading Disclosures) Regulations 2015 (R)

These regulations restrict, dependent on the type of company that you set up, the names that you can use to trade under. They also require you to display your registered company name prominently at the places where you carry out business and show your registered company name and registered office address in all of your company correspondence, documents, and websites.

What is expected of you?

As sourcers, we may not have offices where clients visit, but we do use several different types of documents and letters when dealing with our clients. All correspondence, contracts, forms, and websites must disclose the following:

- ☐ Company name
- ☐ Where in the United Kingdom your company is registered
- ☐ The address of the registered office
- ☐ That it is a 'Ltd' company
- ☐ That it is an investment company (where appropriate)

Governing Body: Local Authority

What are the penalties for failure to comply?

1. The maximum penalty for failing to comply with the regulations is a £1,000 fine plus, for continued breaches, a maximum daily default fine of £100.

Key points to take away

Sourcing Agents:

1. Know which legislation and regulation(s) affect how you can work.

2. Have a good working knowledge of how to be compliant with the legislation or regulation(s).

3. Register for updates on any changes with the appropriate bodies.

Investors:

1. Have a good understanding of your rights as a client.

2. Have a good knowledge of which legislation and regulation(s) your chosen sourcer should be compliant with.

3. Test the sourcers knowledge, this will give you a good indication as to whether they are likely to be compliant.

4. Stay up to date with changes that may affect how you work with your chosen sourcer or for your own protection should anything go wrong.

Chapter 3 – Insurance – Must Have, Should Have & Could Have?

If you own a car, you will know that there are some insurance policies that you are required to have, such as insurance for using the vehicle on the road, and of course, road tax.

When running a business, there are also some insurance policies, which you 'must have', some that you really 'should have' and others that you 'could have'.

Below is a list of the **'must have'**, **'should have'** and **'could have'** insurance policies for your property sourcing business:

Professional Indemnity (PI) Insurance *(Must have)*

This insurance covers your legal liability for any advice that you provide in a professional capacity. It also covers you for liability of breach of professional duty in relation to any service that you provide in exchange for a fee.

It is a requirement of two of the Property Redress Schemes detailed below; although you could choose to join the scheme without requirement for insurance, it is my opinion that it would be irresponsible as I would hope that you wish to portray your company as being professional and trustworthy. Whilst you would always wish to provide the best of service to your clients, should anything go wrong, the business that has adequate insurance stands more chance of having a long-term future than one that doesn't.

The Property Ombudsman (TPO) Scheme – Minimum cover required: £100,000 with a maximum excess of £1,000. If your excess is more than the £1,000 preferred, your insurer must add a clause into your policy. The name on the insurance certificate must match the name on the TPO register for your business.

Property Redress Scheme (PRS) – Minimum cover required: £100,000, there is no excess requirement.

Ombudsman Services Scheme – Does not require proof of Professional Indemnity Insurance for membership. Can issue a financial award of up to £25,000 – As a member, if you reject their decision, you lose the right to the resolution offered but can still make a complaint elsewhere.

Vehicle Insurance *(Must have)*

If you intend to use your own personal vehicle when carrying out property viewings and meetings with potential clients or investors, you must ask your current insurance provider if any amendments are needed to your policy with regard to business use. Whilst your current policy may cover you for travelling to and from work, it may not cover you for full business use.

Don't forget, you may well want to claim mileage allowance for those trips as well as other 'out of pocket' expenses, giving a clear indication that the journey was in fact business related and not personal.

Employers' Liability Insurance *(Must have – if requirement met)*

This insurance covers you if an employee falls ill or is injured as a result of the work that they carry out for you.

The legal requirement for employers to purchase employers' liability insurance was introduced in The Employers' Liability (Compulsory Insurance) Act 1969. This Act requires almost all employers to have a minimum level of insurance cover once they take on their first employee and is enforced by The Health and Safety Executive (HSE).

The minimum level of employers' liability cover is £5million; most reputable insurance providers provide a minimum cover of £10million.

Exceptions to the rule:

- Limited companies: One employee (i.e. you) with greater than 50% of the share capital.

- Unincorporated businesses: Sole Trader or Partnerships where the only employees are close family members (HSE definition of 'close family member': husband, wife, civil partner, father, mother, grandfather, grandmother, stepfather, stepmother, son, daughter, grandson, granddaughter, stepson, stepdaughter, brother, sister, half-brother or half-sister).

- Only employees who are not ordinarily resident in the UK.

Even if you only employ staff occasionally and on a casual basis, temporary or seasonal staff then you must take out cover. If you are not sure, then a guide would be to consider whether you dictate when and where someone works and whether you deduct their income tax and national insurance contributions. If any of your answers were 'yes', then you would probably be counted as an employer.

Failure to have suitable insurance cover can lead to a fine of up to £2,500 per day.

Client Account Insurance *(Must have)*

A client account is a bank account held in the name of the company that it is registered to, but is completely separate from all other accounts linked to that company; the name for this account must include the word 'client' in its title. If you use such an account, then you must have appropriate client account insurance for it.

An independent accountant must audit all transactions from and to this account annually. If you receive or hold clients' money, then you must do so in accordance with the Estate Agents (Accounts) Regulations 1981.

Client money means:

- Money of any currency
- In any format, e.g. cash, cheque, draft or electronic transfer
- Held by a company and is not immediately due and payable on demand to the company for its own account

Such monies must be held in the currency in which it was received unless the client grants permission in writing to change. Most high street banks have the facility to provide a client account upon request; some do not insist on you already having another bank account with them.

If, as a property sourcer or deal packager, you receive a deposit or reservation fee, you MUST use a client account to hold the monies in. (1). Failure to do so could lead to a very large fine (2).

Buildings & Contents Insurance *(Should have)*

Whilst this type of insurance is not compulsory, if you own your own commercial premises, it makes sense to protect them with at least the basic cover for fire and flood and also a policy that includes coverage for your fixtures and fittings.

If you work from home, don't forget that some domestic building and content policies will not provide cover for the running of a business from home, and so it is always best to check with your provider if that is the case and acquire extra cover as required.

Income Protection (IP) Insurance *(Could have)*

This protects you against loss of income due to an inability to work from illness or injury. This is worthwhile considering if you are the sole income provider for your household and may not have the ability to continue to meet payment for your household bills or you have dependents such as children reliant on a certain level of income.

Public Liability Insurance *(Could have)*

This type of insurance is not required by law but covers you against the risk of death, injury, or damage to property suffered by a third party including members of the general public or any other business that works with you. The level of cover available normally starts at around £1million.

If in the process of providing your service you come into contact with members of the public or work with other businesses, it may be worth considering obtaining suitable cover.

Directors' and Officers' (D&O) Liability Insurance *(Could have)*

This protects any directors or other officers of the company from potential claims made against them as a result of decisions or actions that they have taken in the scope of their regular business duties.

The Limited Liability facility of the company only protects the company and the personal assets of the owners if the business fails to be able to meet its financial obligations.

Claims could be made against you or other directors personally as individuals rather than the company itself and enable you to cover the cost of any defence for such claims.

Some examples of Directors being sued personally:

a) Department of Business Innovation and Skills (BIS) brought a disqualification action against two directors of a failed estate agency for continuing to trade when there were no reasonable prospects of creditors being paid.

b) A company agreed to hold a customer's monies in a separate trust account. However, after the company went into liquidation, it was discovered that the monies had not been held in a separate account, and the customer sued the Directors personally for their financial loss.

Key points to take away

Sourcing Agents:

Must Have:

Professional Indemnity ☐
Vehicle (Business Use Cover) ☐
Client Account ☐
Employers Liability (If requirement met) ☐

Should Have:

Buildings and Contents ☐

Could Have:

Public Liability ☐
Income Protection ☐
Directors and Officers Liability ☐

Investors:

Ask the sourcer if they have Professional Indemnity & Client Account Insurance - If their service turns out to be poor you may be able to claim compensation from them - If they don't have any your only recourse may be the 'small claims court' with a resriction on the size of the compensation awarded currently being £10,000 (England and Wales)

Chapter 4 – Are you ready for:
Compulsory Registration and Compliance
or Heavy Fine and Imprisonment?

A significant part of being a property agent is to show that you are professional, trustworthy, reliable, and honest. Professional registrations are just one of the ways that this image can be portrayed, and the ones mentioned below are mandatory for our sector.

1) Property Redress Schemes

The Consumers and Estate Agents Redress Act 2007 requires that all persons or companies carrying out estate agency work (as defined by the Estate Agents Act 1979) be registered with any one of three government recognised property redress schemes currently available in England & Wales:

- The Property Ombudsman (TPO)
- The Property Redress Scheme (PRS)
- Ombudsman Services: Property

The Property Redress Scheme is the only one that is run for profit, it is owned by the insurance company Hamilton Frazer.

Each redress scheme has its own individual 'Code of Practice' and membership compliance expectations; study each one and then decide which scheme is right for you and ensure that you are compliant with your code of practice.

Each redress scheme has various levels of membership available, with varying costs and levels of service provided dependent of which is chosen.

Here is a breakdown of membership levels, service provided and the relevant costs for each:

The Property Ombudsman (TPO) – www.tpos.co.uk

Levels of Registration

a) Registration Only   b) Membership

Fee Structure

Registration only: £195 + VAT per branch per year + one off £50 initial registration fee

Membership: £195 + VAT per branch per year + a one off £50 initial registration fee

Member Compliance Expectations

Registration only: Agree to follow TPO General Membership Obligations

Membership: Agree to follow TPO Codes of Practice

The Property Redress Scheme (PRS) – www.theprs.co.uk

Levels of Registration

a) Entry   b) Enhanced

Fee Structure

Entry: £95 + VAT per branch per year + complaint fee £60 + VAT (Member of body with client protection insurance) otherwise £90 + VAT

Enhanced: £199 + VAT per branch per year (no complaints fee and free access to 24/7 legal helpline)

Member Compliance Expectations

Entry and enhanced: Agree to comply with Ombudsman's decisions should a complaint progress to that stage.

Ombudsman Services: Property – www.ombudsman-services.org

Levels of Registration

Membership

Fee Structure

Initial registration: £150 + VAT per branch per year + complaints case fee £260 + VAT.

Member Compliance Expectations

Agree to follow general membership rules.

When starting out as a new business owner, it is easy to fall into the trap of thinking that registration fees are an expense that you can do without, that no one will notice for a while; if we complete just a couple of deals, no one will know or we are too small for them to bother about us.

Here are several examples of businesses just like yours that thought that they would save a few quid and not register ...

April 2016 – A Darlington lettings and sales agent was fined £3,000 by the local authority for failure to register with an approved redress scheme. *(1)*

November 2015 – Three Darlington agents were fined a total of £8,000 (£2,667 each) by the local authority for failure to register with an approved redress scheme. *(2)*

73

<u>July 2015</u> – Eleven agents in Sheffield were fined in total £37,000 (£3,364 each) by the local authority for failure to register with an approved redress scheme. *(3)*

Your local authority has the ability to fine you up to £5,000 for failure to register with one of the approved redress schemes, a further £5,000 for continued failure to comply and ultimately close your business down.

Or possibly believe that registering with a cheaper option, a lower cost upfront, but running the risk of having to pay if a complaint is made against you, but of course, no one will ever complain about you; will they.

Here are several examples of businesses just like yours that thought no one would ever complain about them...

The Property Ombudsman

A complaint was received from a Vendor (Seller) that the Agent had fabricated evidence of other viewings and offers for their property (£20,000 & £30,000 higher) in order to apply pressure to an existing buyer to close the sale. The existing buyers withdrew their offer, and the sale was lost. Upon completion of an investigation, it was clear that these offers were fictitious, and the Ombudsman awarded the Vendor £650 in compensation for their avoidable aggravation, stress, and inconvenience. *(4)*

Property Redress Scheme

A complaint was received from a buyer that the Agent had misled them as to the size of the property. The buyer complained that a) the agent's floor plan in the sales particulars substantially exaggerated the size of the apartment. The floor plan stated that the size was 100msq when it was actually 80msq b) the information provided by the agent with regard to the size had affected the buyer's decision to purchase, resulting in a difference of end valuation.

Upon completion of an investigation, the Ombudsman awarded compensation of £1,000 to the buyer citing breaches of the Consumer Protection from Unfair Trading Regulations 2008 (CPR's). Although the floor plans had contained a disclaimer, which stated that 'whilst every attempt has been made to ensure the accuracy of the floor plan, the measurements are approximate, and no responsibility is taken for any error, omission or misstatement;' the Ombudsman stated that the disclaimer could not cover such a substantial error in the measurements of the Agent's floor plan. *(5)*

Ombudsman Services

A complaint was received from a buyer that the Agent had failed to disclose that the property they had made an offer on, which was accepted, was Grade II listed.

Upon completion of an investigation, the Ombudsman concluded that the Agent had failed to check the listed status of the building despite the company being aware that there were many properties in that area that were listed properties.

The Agent was required to provide 'an above average award'.

It is a legal requirement to join a government approved redress scheme. Whilst the annual fees may appear to be excessive, or even unnecessary at the beginning of your business journey, the penalties can be high and would no doubt significantly affect the cash flow of even an established business or can result in the ultimate penalty of enforced closure. *(6)*

2) Anti-Money Laundering

As a property sourcing business, you will hopefully receive money from investors in the form of deposits/reservation fees, and on completion of the deal, a sourcing fee. Your investors may possibly reside outside the UK or EU, invest through a company structure or simply as an individual, either way you must be registered for Anti-Money Laundering. The Money Laundering Regulations 2007 require that any business at risk of being used for money laundering by criminals or terrorists have measures in place to minimise that risk. HM Revenue & Customs (HMRC) is currently responsible for the monitoring of this area, having taken over the role in April 2014 from the Office of Fair Trade (OFT).

There is just one level of registration with the following fee structure:

a) Initial Application: £100 + VAT application fee plus £115 per premises registered.

b) Subsequent renewals: £115 + VAT per premises per year.

So, why should you register for anti-money laundering monitoring? Well, the latest report from the National Crime Agency (NCA) estimates that between £36 billion & £90 billion per year is being laundered through the UK (7). The purchasing of property in the UK and overseas as a means to illicit the 'cleaning' of illegally obtained funds is one of the most common methods used by criminal gangs.

Why property? Well, the main advantage is that you can 'clean' large amounts of cash in a single transaction. One of the most common strategies that criminal gangs use is to reserve a property or development site through an agent, just like you, agree to pay a 'holding deposit' or reservation fee and then cancel the purchase, getting a refund of their money back from your 'clean' account; usually into a different account from the one that it originated. Their illegally obtained funds are now clean.

You see, regardless of the original source of their funds, once it has passed through your legitimate account and forwarded to a new account, it is now 'clean.' A refund from a reputable bank account either via electronic transfer or a cheque will never be questioned.

Member compliance expectations are as follows: (see Chapter 6 – for more information):

1. Must register each premises as required for compliance.

2. Must nominate and register a responsible person.

3. Have a written Anti-Money Laundering Policy.

4. Develop and use a risk assessment and management.

5. Have documented procedures.

6. Keep evidence of customer due diligence checks & suspicious activity reports (SAR's).

7. Keep staff training records.

Fail to register and HMRC can do any of the following:

- Issue a warning letter

- Issue unlimited fines

- Issue unlimited civil penalties

- Give a maximum two years imprisonment.

If you think that registering is too much hassle, not necessary for your business, as you know all of your investors, your investors are all from the UK and have UK bank accounts, what could go wrong? This next section is for you ...

Since 2004, £180m+ worth of property in the UK has been brought under criminal investigation as the suspected proceeds of corruption. This is believed to be only the tip of the iceberg, with over 75% of those properties under investigation being held under 'offshore' accounts for secrecy. The average price of a property under criminal investigation in the UK is £1.5m, the minimum is £130,000 (8).

Despite all of this, the figures for suspicious activity reports (SAR's) which should be submitted by agents who suspect money laundering activity accounted for only 0.09% of all reports submitted from October 2014 to September 2015 (9).

In the financial year 2014/15, HMRC issued total fines of £768,000(10) (677 individual penalties) equating to an average of £1,100 per penalty. With the current focus on the property sector in general, do you think that HMRC will decrease or increase their focus on our sector? Well, I firmly believe it will significantly increase, why? The government has announced that it would redouble its efforts on curbing money laundering activity in the UK, and the 4th Money Laundering Directive came into force in June 2015 and will be adopted (Legislation passed – Updated Money Laundering Regulations 2007) in the UK by the deadline of 26th June 2017.

You need to take your Anti-Money Laundering responsibilities seriously, or that decision may not only cost you your business but also the possibility of a 'stretch behind bars.'

Data Protection

Put very simply, the Data Protection Act 1998 regulates the 'processing' of personal data (about living individuals) that includes obtaining, recording, or holding that information. The data can be held in paper or electronic formats, back up drive or cloud-based. The information could have been gathered from a business card given to you at a networking event, a contact form completed and submitted on your website, a message sent to you via social media or an introductory contact email. Once a company processes this information, they are required to register with the Information Commissioners Office (ICO) who are responsible for registering and monitoring of data protection regulation compliance.

There is just one level of registration with the following fee structure:

a) Initial Application: Unless your business has a turnover in excess of £25.9m, you will pay £35 + VAT per year.

Some of the member compliance expectations:

1. Must register each premises as required for compliance.

2. Must nominate & register a responsible person.

3. Follow the eight data protection principles of good information handling: fair and lawful, purposes, adequacy, accuracy, retention, rights, security and international (See Chapter 2 – for more information).

Fail to register, and the ICO can do any of the following:

☐ Issue a maximum fine of £5,000 for failure to register

☐ Should the breach of the regulations be significant, can impose a fine of up to £500,000.

I can hear you saying, "But I only have information on a couple of hundred contacts," "my company is too small for them to be bothered about me" or you may be thinking, "what a complete waste of time and money". Well, before you make that mistake, read some of the examples below, people and businesses just like yours that thought the same thing …

June 2016 – Swansea company fined £350 + costs £497.75 – Failing to Register (11).

April 2016 – Kent Police Force fined £80,000 after sending the accused sensitive details of a woman who had made an accusation of abuse against her former partner (email/postal error) (11).

March 2016 – A company made 168 'cold calls' over a six-month period to people on a list purchased from a third party – most people on the list had already registered with the Telephone Preference Service, opting out from marketing calls - Following several complaints, the ICO issued a fine of £50,000 *(11)*.

We all use personal contact details in our everyday lives; however, when it comes to business, there are regulations governing what we can hold, how we hold it, how long we can hold it, and what we can do with it. It could be a very costly mistake to think that it does not affect you as a sourcing agent or that you do not need to have at least a basic understanding of the regulations and how to be compliant. Have you ever bought a list of potential sellers (supposedly pre-screened) and made some approach phone calls? I know that I did in the early days, and that is all that the company fined £50,000 had done too!

So how much will it cost you to complete the initial compliance steps?

	Initial Cost (Entry) + VAT	Initial Cost (Enhanced) + VAT
Professional Indemnity Insurance - Minimum £100,000: Approx	£300.00*	£300.00*
Property Ombudsman Registration:		
The Property Ombudsman (TPO)	£245.00	£245.00
Property Redress Scheme (PRS)	£120.00**	£199.00
Ombudsman Services	£150.00***	£150.00***
Data Protection	£35.00	£35.00
Anti-Money Laundering	£215.00	£215.00
Total Set up Costs - Min & Max (in region of)	£700.00	£795.00
*Cost of insurance can vary dependent on cover and provider chosen		
**Plus £80.00 + VAT for each complaint		
***Plus £260 + VAT for each complaint		

Key points to take away

Sourcing Agents:

You have a responsibility not only to yourselves but also to your clients to operate in an ethical, legal and honest manner. These three simple steps below will set your business apart from the vast majority that currently operate in the UK who may not even know that these exist.

1. Must register with any 1 of 3 Government approved Redress Schemes in England & Wales.

2. Must register for Data Protection with the ICO.

3. Must register for Anti-Money Laundering with HMRC.

4. Must have at least a basic understanding of the steps needed for compliance with each of the above.

Investors:

When you use a sourcing agent you are not only putting your trust in someone that you may only just have met but also quite often, large sums of hard earned/saved cash. If you do not carry out YOUR due diligence on them and they are not registered with an approved Redress Scheme your only recall for compensation would be through the small claims courts with a possible maximum award of £10,000. Would £10,000 in compensation cover your costs on any of your deals had they gone seriously wrong?

1. If thinking of using a sourcing agent check that they are registered with the following:
   a) A Government approved Property Redress Scheme
   b) Data Protection (ICO)
   c) Anti-Money Laundering (HMRC)

2. Ask to speak directly to at least one investor that they have worked with and sourced deals for.

3. Have at least a basic understanding of how they should be complying with each of the compulsory registration bodies, that way they are less likely to be able to deceive you into believing that they are more experienced than they actually are.

Chapter 5 – How to Avoid Lost Fees and Fines

I hope that just like me you feel that you want to portray your business in the most professional and positive manner. At this time, I believe that it would be unusual if a property sourcer used the full list of letters, guides, contracts, and forms described later in this chapter. However, I feel that by doing so, more and more investors will migrate to those property sourcers who are working to these high standards.

Most investors are not used to this approach and may, in the beginning, query the level of information being asked for. However, if you clearly explain the reasons for doing so and why it is beneficial to them, they will come to appreciate the benefits of working with you. For example, professional registrations and insurances bring added assurance for the investor should anything go wrong; also, your knowledge of compliance matters along with a high level of knowledge for the industry in general, portray an exceptionally level of professionalism. It will also be of considerable assistance that from June 2016 ALL estate agents, even if contracted to the seller MUST carry out due diligence on the buyer as well; something that in the past they have never been legally obliged to do.

To achieve all of that, you need to have created professional looking, legally checked agreements, contracts, and client forms. Why legally checked? Well, because if a client signs an agreement with you and then something goes wrong, if the original contract was not legally binding, contained errors, was misleading or contained unfair statements or clauses, then you might well lose any legal case for compensation or being able to claim your fees as expected.

The lists of documents below are what, as a company, we use; some of them are either/or, it is not necessary to use all of them. However, should a complaint be made or an investigation be initiated with regard to your company and its processes, having these documents and other processes in place could help to prove that you have behaved fairly with regard to the vendor, property or investor and that marketing, contracts, and due diligence checks have been completed within regulation guidelines.

Seller

Information Gathering Forms

a) **Task Check List** – A tick box form that indicates which documents were sent to the seller/vendor, date sent, date returned signed and completed, and also if a copy is held on file, and

b) **Personal Data Capture Form** – Collects relevant personal information from the seller/vendor, used to obtain information that will be needed for confirming identification, etc.

Contracts & Agreements

a) **Option Agreement** – Legally binding contract signed by you and the seller, detailing the property or site in question, price agreed, and timescale to achieve a sale. Usually exchanged with a payable £1 fee, or

b) **Sole Agency Agreement** – Seller signs this contract to state that they agree to your terms and conditions of service giving you 'Sole' rights to sell on their behalf for a fixed period of time, used if a seller refuses to agree to a fixed purchase price for the 'option' or where they prefer a standard estate agency type contract, and

c) **Misdescription Disclaimer** – A form, which you ask the seller to sign after they have seen your marketing materials for their property, in which they confirm that all information used in your marketing, is accurate.

Guides and Letters

a) **Company: Who we are and what we do?** – This is optional, but explains who you are, what you do, and should also include details of your redress scheme registered with, etc.

b) **Confirmation of Instruction Letter** – Used in conjunction with the 'Sole Agency Agreement', a letter, which asks the seller to confirm that they give you permission to market their property or site, and

c) **Guidance for consumers (Sellers)** – The TPO provide an information sheet that can be given to a seller, check whether your ombudsman provides a similar document.

d) **Company: Complaints Procedure** – This is optional, but property redress schemes insist that you have an 'In-house complaints' policy and procedure in place and available to view upon request; some companies have a link to these on their website.

Property

Information Gathering Forms

a) **Property Detail Capture Form** - A form that collects relevant information about the property or site, such as number of reception rooms, bedrooms, bathrooms, details of gardens, garage or off road parking; this should provide a full description of the property, etc. – Ensure that you include anything that might affect the value of the property or site or cause the purchase to fail, for example, a history of flooding or serious structural flaws – Consider including a final question such as '… can you think of anything that a buyer might want to know…?' and

b) **Offer Record Form** – A form which holds details of ALL offers made on the property or site including date and whether accepted by the seller/vendor.

Investor

Due Diligence

a) **Task Check List** - A tick box form that indicates which documents were sent to the investor, date sent, date returned signed and completed, and if a copy is held on file, and

b) **Personal/Company Data Capture Form** - A form that collects relevant information about an individual investor, shareholder or company. Any information that you need to confirm their identification and also that of the company, and

c) **Investment Type Pro-forma** – A form, which gathers detailed information about the investors' short, mid & long-term investment goals, preferred investment types, geographical areas and also funds available for each project and overall investment amount available, and

d) **Money Laundering Risk Assessment Score Form** – A form that you must complete to show how you have assessed the risk from working with your client, and

e) **Money Laundering Risk Assessment Conclusion Notes** – Notes to back up your decision to work with (or not) your client based on the risk posed from completing the ML Risk Assessment form (d).

Contracts & Agreements

a) **Terms & Conditions** – A contract that the investor signs that states that they agree to your terms and conditions.

b) **Deal Introduction/Sourcing Fee Agreement** – An agreement sent to the investor who signs to say that they agree to pay your (specified) fee for that specific project.

Guides

a) **Business: Who we are and what do we do** - An explanation of who you are, what you do, and this should also include details of your redress scheme and who it is registered with, etc.

b) **Guidance for Consumers: Investors** - The TPO provide an information sheet that can be given to a buyer, and

c) **Company: Complaints Procedure** – Some Property Redress Schemes insist that you have one in place.

I can hear you say: "What, you have to be joking!"

No joke – whilst I admit that I have 'tweaked' our documents, letters, and contracts, before I started to trade deals ALL of the legally required basics were in place and have only been changed over the years so that we remain compliant with any changes to the regulations or changing requirements of the property ombudsman scheme that we are members of.

Some questions that you may have:

i)   Our initial set up costs (gradually over a five-year period) for ALL of our contracts and terms and conditions including for the website were in the region of £4,000.

ii)   Yes, we have our contracts and agreements checked annually by an experienced contracts solicitor. It would make your life easier if you work on recommendation with regard to a competent and reliable solicitor.

iii)   Annual cost for checks? Ours are in the region of £500 to £750 (These costs could be higher or lower dependent on where you are in the country and the solicitor used).

iv)   Are these checks really necessary? We feel that these checks are absolutely necessary as laws and regulations change, and you need to know that your documentation continues to be legally compliant, fair and easy for the client to understand; only a qualified solicitor experienced in contract law could assure you of this.

We, of course, also monitor for any changes to the regulations so that appropriate changes can be made in the interim if required.

So, what would the 'pain factor' be should you ignore all of this? As the title of the chapter states, you either comply or you could face unlimited fines and or imprisonment of up to 14 years. You could be guilty of breaches of contract and marketing regulations, data protection, and Money Laundering to mention just a few, but also potentially the loss of your fees, for which you have worked hard for sometimes over several months. If you ever have a problem in getting your investor to pay your fee and there is a problem with your contracts or agreements, then you might have a major problem in getting your fee at all.

Not having legally checked documents, contracts, or agreements in place could prove to be much more expensive in the long term than having paid for them to be professionally checked in the first place.

Key points to take away

Sourcing Agents:

1. Ensure that you have accurate, clearly written, fair contracts and agreements for both sellers and investors, preferably legally checked.

2. To set your self apart from the crowd, provide guides on relevant subjects, a brief overview of your company, one from a sellers' perspective and another from the investors. An EPC guide for the seller or money laundering information sheet for the investor.

3. Have a system in place so that when documents are sent out to a client, you can record what was sent, date sent, to whom, date returned, date completed and if you have a copy on file etc.

4. Regularly check through your guides, letters, agreements and contracts. Are they still up to date with current legislation? Consider having them checked by an experienced commercial contract solicitor every 12 to 18 months to ensure continuing compliance.

Investors:

1. When considering working with a property sourcer ask them if you can see examples of their contracts and agreements prior to agreeing to work with them.

2. Are the contracts and agreements easy to read; crucially, do you understand them?

3. If you have any queries about aspects of any of the documents, could they answer the questions posed to your satisfaction? They should have a basic understanding of what their contracts and agreements cover.

4. Does the property sourcer provide you with relevant guides such as money laundering etc.?

5. Do you feel that they appear to be professional in their approach to you?

Chapter 6 – Client Due Diligence (CDD) – Investor, Seller & Property

The majority of the due diligence process that is covered in this chapter is related to money laundering and other criminal activity. Whilst this chapter gives you a good basic grounding in the subject, I recommend that you add to the knowledge contained here by reading the many guides that are available on the web and any other material that is relevant to the subject in relation to the property sector. There are some useful links to be found on both the reference and resource pages at the rear of this book.

Investor

The Money Laundering legislation and associated guidance all state that the identity of a person and/or company must be verified as soon as practicable after first contact between you or your company and them, in this case, the investor. 'As soon as practicable' will depend on how quickly your client wants to progress through the registration and due diligence process and be able to purchase a deal from you. If you have a deal that they are aware of and wish to progress with, then obviously they may wish to speed up the process in order to secure the deal; whereas an investor for whom you have nothing immediately available that is of interest to them may take more time in completing the process.

Although it may be tempting to rush the due diligence on an investor in order to complete a purchase and receive your fee, this would be unwise. Should it later become apparent that the transaction was, in fact, used to launder monies, as you will have already read in chapter 2, the punishment can be severe with an unlimited fine and up to 14 years in prison for serious offences.

You are expected to apply your professional judgment to make an informed decision about when, in your line of business and with your risk exposure, it would be prudent to carry out these checks. Client due diligence must be applied to all new clients before you provide services to them. You will need to decide for yourself when your relationship has reached a stage where due diligence should be commenced before progressing further. As always, keep clear records to document your decision and justification for it.

If for whatever reason, verification of the identity of a client cannot be carried out, then the business must be declined. If in the process of declining this business, a staff member suspects money laundering or engaging in terrorist financing, this suspicion must be reported in the usual way, this is covered in more detail later in this chapter.

I have broken potential clients down to the three main types of investor that you are likely to come across:

1) Individual
2) Company
3) Partnership

There are, of course, other client entity types that you may come across, for example, a Trust or Charity; for these, you would have to research as to what individual criteria, if any, are required for proving identity.

It doesn't matter whether your potential client is an individual or a company; there are seven main elements to your client due diligence process:

1) Assessing the Risk
2) Verifying Identity
3) Knowing your Client's Business

4) Ongoing Monitoring
5) Record Keeping
6) Internal Suspicion Report
7) Disclosure to Authorities

Let's take a look in more detail at each of these areas:

1) Assessing the Risk

There are no set number of levels of due diligence stipulated within the regulations or guides. The number of levels that you use will depend on the variety of clients that you deal with on a day-to-day basis. For example, if the vast majority of your clients are 'resident UK nationals' then your main due diligence check level may be 'Simple'; however, it is always wise to have an 'Enhanced' due diligence level, just in case you are approached by a client from a higher risk group (explained later in the chapter.).

Your risk assessment should be company wide, which means that everyone within your company should have access to and an understanding of what is required of them in their particular role. You must be able to justify your decisions made, using your 'Risk Model'.

I will share with you the two different levels that as a company we decided to use:

Simple:

You must be able to show that through your risk assessment process you established that the business relationship and transactions resulting from that relationship would pose a lower risk of money laundering. However, you must also show that you continue to monitor the situation for any changes in strategy, funds available or any other suspicious activity irrespective of the results of your original due diligence checks completed.

These are the two groups of potential clients that would fall into the 'Simple' due diligence category:

a) UK or EU National: Residing in UK or EU, with a UK Bank account, or,
b) Company: Registered, with a simple ownership structure, operating within the UK, with a UK bank account.

Enhanced:

Again, you must be able to show that through your risk assessment process you established the level of risk of money laundering and show that you continue to monitor the situation for any changes irrespective of your original due diligence checks completed.

These are the three groups of potential clients that would fall into the 'Enhanced' due diligence category:

a) Anyone else, but must include:
   i) Any client not met face to face, and/or
   ii) A Politically Exposed Person (PEP) (1) - Someone that has been entrusted with a prominent public function, or a relative or known associate of that person

We have structured our due diligence levels in this way to keep our decision process simple and easy to follow. You must develop a process that reflects the particular types of clients that you provide a service for and how you wish to work.

2) Verifying Identity

Individual - Simple

An individual, not buying under a company structure, who falls within the 'Simple' risk assessment level as mentioned earlier.

Identity checks to prove:

- Show client is who they say they are
- Show client lives where they say they do

Simple verification should include:

- Name
- Address
- Date of Birth

These can be obtained from either a valid passport or valid photo identity driving licence.

Individual – Enhanced

An individual, not buying under a company structure, who falls within the 'Enhanced' risk assessment level mentioned earlier.

Identity checks to prove:

- Name
- Address
- D.O.B
- Gender
- Nationality

Enhanced verification can be obtained from a valid passport, valid photo identity driving licence or a utility bill, which is less than three months old. Please note that you MUST NOT use only one form of identification to prove ALL of the above points, e.g. name, address, D.O.B, gender and nationality. We use either passport or photo driving licence for name, date of birth, and nationality but use a utility bill for confirmation of address.

For a foreign client (non UK or EU resident), you could choose to use the services of a regulated official from their country of origin, such as a solicitor. They can confirm the client's identity by carrying out the face-to-face checks that you are unable to complete. Do not forget to carry out due diligence on that company and the individual who provides the confirmation email or letter.

Just as an extra layer of checks, we use social media, for example, Facebook & LinkedIn. Check that the person you met and the details from their identification document(s) match those on social media profiles; some people even include their home address within their profile.

Company (Listed) – Simple

The objective of your due diligence process on a company is to prove:

- That the company structure is simple and opaque, not a company owned by another company owned by another company owned by a group. Where the company shareholders are ALL named individual people with various levels of shares allocated to them.

- To identify how the company is structured, key documents for Limited Liability Companies are a Certificate of Incorporation, Annual Return (AR), and Memorandum and Articles of Association. All of these can be viewed, and some can be downloaded from Companies House.

Unlike with the single step process for an individual investor, once you have identified how the company is structured, you will also need to find and identify the beneficial owners, those who have control over the company and its funds, also known as shareholders. Verifying their identities in the same way as you would for an individual investor as described earlier in this chapter.

Your ability to be able to identify the person(s) with beneficial ownership of a UK registered company should be easier now through the use of the 'People with Significant Control' (PSC) register (2). You can now access all of the information necessary to identify all PSC's directly from the Companies House Website (3)

To correctly identify and verify the company, you need to obtain the following:

- Company Name
- Registered Number
- Registered Address
- Business Address
- Names of ALL Shareholders
- Individual identity check(s) on at least the main shareholder or controller
- Identify the reason for the business relationship, e.g. they wish to invest in property.

It is essential that you link your contact/client to the company and that they have permission to carry out business with you on behalf of the company and ALL of the other shareholders if applicable. A letter from a shareholder can be obtained as proof of permission, but you MUST carry out identification checks on the authoriser.

You MUST identify at least the beneficial owner of the company, the shareholder with the largest percentage share, before proceeding with a business relationship.

Company (Listed) - Enhanced

The objectives are the same as 'Simple' above, but more in-depth:

- Verify identity of one or more Director(s) – Specifically Managing Director
- Verify identity of Shareholders with 25% or higher control
- Verify Agent/Contact Person linked to company

Directors do not fall within the definition of beneficial owner simply by virtue of their directorship but would do so if they were also shareholders who meet the criteria set above.

Some questions to ask yourself:

- Is the company registered in structure known for lack of transparency or corrupt? (A company with a complex structure or registered in a so-called 'Tax Haven') (4)
- Is it linked to a Politically Exposed Person (PEP)?
- Are its main activities generally vulnerable to money laundering? Some examples:
  o Professional Advisors – Accountants, Solicitors, and Stockbrokers
  o Gambling Businesses – Casinos, etc.
  o Financial Institutions – Travel Agents
  o Antique Dealers, Jewellers or Designers
  o Any Internet-based business
- Carry out individual identity checks on ALL shareholders.

As before, it is essential that you link your contact/client to the company and that they have permission to carry out business with you on behalf of the company and ALL the shareholders; a letter from a shareholder can be obtained as proof of permission, but you MUST carry out identification checks on the authoriser.

Once again, you **MUST** identify the beneficial owner of the company.

Partnerships - Simple

Partnerships should be verified to standards similar to those used for companies. The key document for partnership identification is the 'Deed of Partnership'.

Where the number of partners is small, the recommended policy is to verify the identity of all partners. For larger partnerships refer to the 'Deed of Partnership' to determine who has effective control.

It is legal for a Partnership to exist without using a 'Deed of Partnership', this is known as 'partnership at will'; if this is the case, all partners' identities must be individually verified.

Partnerships - Enhanced

For partnerships assessed as requiring enhanced due diligence, you should obtain the following:

- Individual verification of identity for the individual with whom you are dealing
- For larger partnerships, individual identity verification for one or more of the partners including the managing partner
- For smaller partnerships, individual identity verification of ALL the partners

As before, it is essential that you link your contact/client to the partnership and that they have permission to carry out business with you on behalf of ALL partners; a letter from a partner can be obtained as proof of permission, but you MUST carry out identification checks on the authoriser.

It can be difficult to identify the person(s) with beneficial ownership of a UK registered company when those shares are in foreign hands. There are some sites, which may assist:

☐ The Land Registry Overseas Companies Data – Ownership of Property and Land in the UK (5)

☐ Pan-European Beneficial Ownership Register – Soon to be released list of European beneficial owners of companies (6)

Where a wholly foreign owned company approaches you, the site below provides links to lists of registered companies in various countries around the world:

☐ Companies House – Overseas Registries (7)

Evidence Types

There are three different types of evidence that can be used:

- Documentary – Passport, Driving Licence, and utility bill, etc.
- Data or information from a reliable source (Government Department)
- Electronic – 192.com or Land Registry for address confirmation or Companies House for company verification

If your client is considered to be 'low risk', you can accept as evidence, funds present in a bank or building society account regulated in the UK or EU, providing that account is in the sole name of the client or if husband & wife or partners, joint names; this is known as a 'Source of Funds' concession. However, you must record in your records why you decided that this was sufficient.

Other documents acceptable for proof of identity:

- Passport
- Photo driving licence
- Instrument of a court appointment – Letter of appointment at court
- Current council tax bill or statement
- Utility bill (less than three months old)
- Current bank or credit card statement – UK accounts (must be original documents, not printed from the internet)
- Home & contents insurance document (must show client address & name)
- Letters from accountants, solicitors, doctors, dentists or prescription label

Certified Copies (Identity documents)

When you have seen original documents and taken copies, you MUST then certify them. If accepting copies from the client, you must make sure that they have already been certified appropriately. You cannot accept an uncertified copy and then certify it unless the original document is provided as well.

Those permitted to certify copies for UK clients are:

- Regulated or professional individuals covered by the Money Laundering Regulations. This will include your own staff, although you may choose to designate that responsibility to particular members of staff.

- Employees of Government departments.

Those permitted to certify copies for non-UK clients are:

- Staff within the embassy, consulate or high commission of the country that has issued the document

- Senior officials within the account-opening organisation (e.g. UK Bank)

- Lawyers

The person who takes the copy of the document should certify the copy by writing on it words to the effect of:

'I have seen the original document and this copy is a full and accurate copy of that original'.

If the identity document bears a photograph, they should add:

'Which in itself bears a good likeness of the holder'.

They should then:

- Sign the copy
- Date of their signature
- Clearly print their name
- Contact details.

Electronic Verification Methods:

As well as looking at paper proof of identity, you can also look at online sources to verify identity, such as:

- Electoral Register – www.192.com/people
- Credit reference agencies – Call Credit, Equifax, and Experian – Can be used to confirm client identification.
- Public records database e.g. County Court judgements
- Companies House – registered companies only
- Yellow pages or similar directories.
- Due Diligence check companies – There are many online companies offering this service, the cost can vary, and of course, ensure that you understand how they carry out their checks and where information is sourced; you are still responsible if checks are flawed. It is not wise to rely solely on electronic checks made by such companies. I will be carrying out research into such companies in the near future and may well publish my findings as to how they work, costs for services, and ease of use, etc.
- Social Media sites – LinkedIn & Facebook

These electronic checks for due diligence do not need prior permission from your client; however, you do need to inform them that such checks may be carried out, possibly indicating this clearly in your company information sheet or other documentation issued to a prospective client.

Guarding Against Forged Identity Documents

In our modern world, the chances of coming across forged documentation is a distinct possibility and one that all companies should take seriously. In the battle against forged identification documents, it is imperative that the staff responsible for client due diligence are trained to look for signs that may indicate a forged or fraudulent document.

Here are some examples that may prove useful:

1. Older style British driving licences:

- Have a faint *'COPY'* watermark that shows up boldly when the document is photocopied.

2. The driving licence number:

- The first letters are the first five characters of your surname – If your surname is less than five characters then the remaining spaces will be filled with the figure 9 e.g. MAN99

- The first and last numbers indicate the year of birth.

- The second and third numbers are the month of birth with either a '0' or '1' added for a male or a '5' or '6' added for a female replacing the first digit.

- The fourth and fifth digits indicate the day of birth

See image of a driving licence below:

JONES558240SA9TO

This can be broken down as follows:

JONES – The first five letters of surname

558240SA9TO– Year of Birth: 1950

558240SA9TO - Gender: Female

558240SA9TO - Month of Birth: August

558240SA9TO - Day of Birth: 24th

558240SA9TO – These are first name initials (if only one it will be followed by a 9 e.g. S9)

558240SA9TO – These are DVLA computer check digits for their use only

Check if the information provided by your client matches other identity documents provided, e.g. gender, D.O.B., nationality, and home address, etc. The above information is also contained in Non-British National passports.

Remote Clients

The more 'remote' your client is, the more checks are needed, see table below:

Client	No of Documents to Prove Name	No of Documents to Prove Address
UK National – Living in UK	1	1
UK National – Living Abroad	1	2
EU National – Living in UK	1	2
EU National – Living in Home Country	1	2
Other Foreign National - Living in UK	2	2
Other Foreign National - Living Elsewhere	2	3

It is the norm in other countries to use 'PO Box' numbers as a postal address, these are NOT considered to be legal postal addresses in the UK, and in these cases you would need to carry out enhanced due diligence. Under these circumstances, the buildings and contents insurance policy may be helpful as it is a requirement that it states the address to which it refers to for the policy.

Exemptions from verification or identity requirements

- Existing clients – Those already known personally – Obviously if you are already working with an investor that you do not know personally and you have not carried out checks on them it makes sense to do so as soon as possible to update your records.

- Clients through acquisition (another sourcing agent) – No need to verify identity as long as identity records are supplied at the time of any acquisition and a warranty is given by the seller that the identities of all acquired clients have been verified, and your organisation undertakes sample testing to ensure that this is the case.

Introductions by 3rd Parties

What are introductions and who are 3rd parties?

An introduction is where another person or company introduces you to a client and provides evidence of their due diligence findings or 'vouches' for them as an individual to allow you to progress a business relationship. A 3rd party is the individual or company that makes the introduction.

For example, as a property sourcer you may receive an enquiry for a deal that you currently have available from another sourcing agent, who represents an investor registered with them. In this case, how could you carry out due diligence on that investor? It is unlikely in the short term that the other sourcing agent will hand over the investor's contact details for you to deal with them directly, although they may agree to as long as you sign a non-disclosure and/or non-circumvention agreement.

However, before commencing a business relationship, you must ensure that due diligence, at least to the same level as your own has been carried out and the sourcing agent must, therefore, provide you with the following information:

- Provide upon request, any information that the introducer found during their due diligence, and
- On request, to forward immediately, copies of any identity, verification, and other relevant documents that the introducer gathered during their due diligence process.

It is also possible that your client may have a relationship with a company regulated by the UK Financial Conduct Authority (FCA), such as a solicitor or accountant, on whom you may be able to rely on for an introduction, provided that the organisation consents to you relying on them.

If the introducing entity is based anywhere other than the UK, it must be subject to mandatory professional registration recognised by law and supervised for compliance under any current Money Laundering Directive. Therefore, your first step in deciding whether or not to rely on an introduction from such an entity is to confirm that the entity is, in fact, eligible to act as an introducer in this way. You should check its existence and status with the regulatory and supervisory agencies, as well as keeping a full record of your findings.

The ultimate responsibility for verifying the identity of a client lies with your organisation, and so regardless of the status of the introducing entity, if you are at all unsure about the standard or reliability of the introduction, you should undertake full identity checks yourself.

Ensure that the introducer has applied at least the same level of due diligence that your company would and also that the level of their due diligence that was applied with that client was at an appropriate level, e.g. not simple when enhanced was required.

Certificates for 3rd Party Introductions

The Joint Money Laundering Steering Group (JMLSG) provide blank introduction certificates which you can use as they are, or adapt for use within your own company (8).

Is Reliance on 3rd Parties for Information a Safe Way to Work?

As with all strategies that are reliant on a third party, there are advantages and disadvantages.

Advantages:

- Reduced costs
- Time saving
- Clients not constantly asked for identity verification

Disadvantages:

- Responsibility remains with you and your organisation
- Must still assure yourselves that 3rd party client due diligence is at least as good as yours and carried out at the correct level, e.g. simple or enhanced

You have to make a judgement call as to whether you will rely on

3rd party due diligence at all or take each case on its own merits.

3) Knowing Your Client's Business

In order to show that you really know your clients business, including their short, mid, and long-term goals, you must go beyond the verification of the identity of the individual or company. To show that you have a good understanding of the nature of their business, you will need to understand the following:

1. What is the individual or company looking to achieve? For example, do they want to:
   a) Purchase 10 X 2 bedroom buy to let properties in the next two years?
   b) Find a plot of land with planning permission for residential development?
   c) Build up a £1m property portfolio within 10 years?

2. For what purpose do they wish to utilise your services? For example:
   a) To source investment property(s) or site(s)?
   b) To source and manage a portfolio?
   c) To source and manage a residential or commercial development?

3. Why did they choose to work with you and not anyone else?
   a) On recommendation from another client?
   b) Your apparent professionalism & high levels of compliance?
   c) From research and responses to questions posed directly to you?

Also get clarity on the following:

1. Where did their funds come from?

2. When were they received?
3. In what form were they received?

You will need to validate the above information where you can, for example:

☐ Received through inheritance – Acquire a copy of the letter from the Executors showing the amount paid, also a copy of their bank statement showing that amount of money being received and confirming whom from.

☐ Received through the sale of a business – Acquire a copy of the completion statement from their solicitor, also a copy of their bank statement showing that amount of money being received and confirming whom from.

☐ Received through the sale of a former investment property – Acquire a copy of the completion statement from their solicitor, also a copy of their bank statement showing that amount of money being received and confirming whom from.

☐ Received through the release of cash from a pension – Obtain a copy of their pension release document, also a copy of their bank statement showing that amount of money being received and confirming whom from.

☐ They simply saved up over a period of time – Obtain bank statements for the past six months to show their salaries going into the account and the gradual increase in funds.

There will be cases where physical evidence may be difficult or sometimes impossible to produce, for example, where it is claimed that the money was a gift from a relative received during their life but now deceased for many years. In such cases, you must assess each situation on its own merits and decide whether there is a potential risk that needs to be looked into further or you believe that the risk is minimal, as always, document your reasoning for whichever decision you come to.

If your client is being assessed under the 'simple' process then any monies that are being held in a UK bank or Building Society can be accepted with no further action, but you must document your reasons for doing this.

A couple of simple points to bear in mind with regard to proof of source of funds:

☐ Does the client's explanations for the source of funds make sense?
☐ Does the explanation seem reasonable?

By understanding all of this, you will be in a better position to spot any sudden changes in strategy or increases in funds available. For example, if your client originally stated that they wished to purchase two buy to let terraced properties per year for three years with a maximum value of £75,000 per property and provided you with proof of funds and also the source of those funds, but suddenly contacted you stating that they now wanted you to source a large development site for them up to a value of £500,000, then the alarm bells should start to ring, and whilst it may be completely innocent, they may have come into an inheritance or even won the lottery, but you MUST carry out further investigation as to the source of the new funds.

As a company, we have experienced some reluctance from investors during the early stages of our relationship, to provide all of the information that is necessary for full checks to be completed. This is completely understandable, as I would not wish to share personal financial information with a complete stranger; would you?

Because of this understandable reluctance, we have taken steps to divide our registration process into smaller segments; these can be completed in a time frame of the client's choosing, but of course, they cannot purchase a deal until ALL due diligence checks have been completed.

Our adapted registration and due diligence segments are as follows:

- ☐ Getting to know you and client investment strategy information
- ☐ Personal identification confirmation
- ☐ Financial due diligence

This reduces the amount of information that we ask for at each stage and can be spaced out to suit the client's comfort with the overall process.

Here are the process stages that we have recently adopted with an explanation for each:

- ☐ Stage 1: Initial contact could possibly be via an exchange of emails or a Facebook/LinkedIn message. There may be a sharing of information between you about your potential clients' investment goals and the services that you could potentially provide. They may provide you with an email address for further communication, or for you to send some information to them about your company and how you work and the services that you can provide.

- ☐ Stage 2: Take time to understand what your investor wants, the types of investment that they are interested in, e.g. BTL, HMO's, commercial conversions, or land for development. Gain a good understanding of their short, mid and long-term goals; in other words, get to 'know your client'. Explain about your registration and due diligence process, what is involved, why it has to be completed and approximate timescales. Point out the benefits of working with a fully compliant property sourcer (professional accountability, insurance and ombudsman registration, etc.) You might also mention some of the potential drawbacks of using a sourcer who has no understanding of the legislation and regulations (potential loss of money, unlikely to have insurance, etc.). This stage may be spread over a couple of days, several weeks, or even months, dependent on the individual investor.

☐ Stage 3: If the investor is happy to progress and provide you with some initial personal information, then this is the time to begin the registration process. It is at this stage that we would also ask for proof of identification and then carry out due diligence to confirm the information provided. Upon completion of this stage, we agree to send the investor 'headline' information only of any projects that we feel may fit their criteria; it would include: type of investment, location, and any key financial figures.

☐ Stage 4: When an investor requests further information on a project that they feel is of interest to them, that is the time when we ask them to read through and sign our 'Terms of Business Agreement'. This document sets out how we work including when payment of our fee is expected, also both a non-disclosure and non-circumvention clause. It is important that your investor signs this agreement or your equivalent before you provide them with full details or direct access to the property or site for viewing, as failure to do so could lead to them attempting to go behind your back and deal directly with the seller to cut you out; without this or a similar agreement being signed, you may have no legal re-course.

☐ Stage 5: If your investor is happy with the project and wishes to put forward an offer, it is at this stage, if not completed earlier, that you must go through the financial due diligence stage, which consists of acquiring not only proof of funds but also proof of the source of those funds.

☐ Stage 6: Your investor has fully completed registration

including the getting to know you, personal identification process and the financial due diligence process. At this stage, you are in a position where you can send full details of projects and progress to purchase without further checks. It should be noted that you are expected to monitor your clients for changes in investment behaviour or sudden increases in funds available.

4) Ongoing Monitoring

The initial due diligence checks that we have gone through earlier in this chapter are just the beginning of the process, it is a part of the mandatory client due diligence process that you must monitor your clients.

The regulation states that you should be 'scrutinising transactions' to ensure that they are consistent with your 'Knowledge of the Client' and in keeping with the information that you previously collated during the initial due diligence process.

Some of the things that you should be monitoring for are:

☐ Changes in client circumstances
☐ Changes in business structure
☐ Changes to sums of money available
☐ Changes in regulation that affect your due diligence levels for that client

The regulations do not state that you need to renew identification documents due to them expiring, for example, passport, or address due to a client moving house. However, if following a house move there is a change in activity with regard to the services that you provide or an increase in funds available, then you must investigate and update your due diligence for that client.

For any clients that are considered to be of 'higher risk', then such things as name changes due to marriage or divorce should be evidenced so as to link the old and new names together on their file, e.g. copy of marriage certificate or decree absolute.

It might be a good idea to consider a timetable for regular reviews of your clients based on their 'Risk' status. See the table below as an example:

	Low Risk	High Risk
Review ID:	Every 3-4 years	Annually
Review CDD:	Annually	Every 3-5 months

A review may only be a matter of confirming that the information already held is still accurate and sufficient for purpose. If the review reveals changes, then it may be necessary to increase the frequency of future reviews.

As always, record that a review has taken place, any new information or changes that have come to light. Here are some significant events, which should 'trigger' a review:

☐ An unusual transaction, out of keeping with previous activity
☐ A change of 'contact person' linked to a company
☐ Unexpected cancellation of a service, e.g. request refund

Regular checks of the PEP or Government Consolidated Sanctions list (9) to check that your client has either been added or removed Specific warning signals for estate agency type businesses:

☐ Property sales which are significantly higher or lower than the current market value, or

☐ A buyer who shows little interest in the details or condition of the property, or

- Buyers who appear to have to consult someone else before making a decision, or

- Wanting a fast resale for no good reason, or

- Resale of a property(s) following refurbishment without knowing where funds had come from, or

- Requests to accept cash as payment or deposit through a client account, or

- Receipt of an expected payment but from an unexpected source, e.g. different bank account from that originally stated.

In general, there are several sites that can be checked with regard to sanctions lists and PEP's; please refer to the Reference and Resource pages at the back of this book.

Please note: even if your fee is being paid by the seller, that does not mitigate you from carrying out due diligence on the buyer; even if those checks will eventually also be carried out by a solicitor or finance company.

5) Record Keeping

Record Formats

For client identification, you must keep:

- Originals or certified copies of the identity document(s) used to verify identity, or

- A record of where these originals or certified copies are kept, or
- Information about how the originals or copies can be obtained

- References to the documents e.g. Passport Number, date and place of issue can only be completed if the original documents have been seen

Please note:

- You cannot accept a mobile phone bill or any documents printed from the Internet that are not the original documents.

- If you cannot complete client due diligence checks, you must NOT act for that client and dependent on the reason for the failure, should consider an 'internal' report to your MLRO.

- If a couple is investing, checks must be completed on both.

- If non-photographic evidence is accepted you must also obtain proof of both address and DOB.

It is important to note that: Records for verification of client identity must be kept for at least five years from the date of the end of the relationship with the client. It is anticipated that UK Money Laundering Regulations will be adapted at some stage in the future to allow some records to be kept for up to 10 years.

6) Internal Suspicion Report – Money Laundering Reporting Officer (MLRO)

As a part of your compliance with the Money Laundering Regulations, you must nominate a Money Laundering Reporting Officer or MLRO. When a member of staff is dealing with a client and becomes suspicious about them or their activity, then they should follow your company's 'Internal Reporting Procedure' which usually states that they submit an Internal Suspicion Report to their MLRO.

Money Laundering offences in the UK are set around the following terms:

'Knowing'   'Suspecting'   'Reasonable grounds to know or suspect'

Upon receiving such a report, the MLRO must decide whether to submit a Suspicious Activity Report (SAR) (10) to the National Crime Agency (NCA) (11) on behalf of the company and ask for consent before beginning or carrying on providing professional services to that client.

If you work alone, then you are automatically the MLRO. Failure to make a report is a criminal offence.

You need to have processes in place that are appropriate for the size and structure of your company, as well as taking into account the money laundering risk that your business may face carrying out its day to day activities.

You should keep records if any unusual activity is noticed with regard to one of your clients and there are reasonable grounds for suspicion, even if it turns out to be 'unfounded'. This will make it much easier for you to defend your actions and decision-making process should there be a future investigation, than if you had recorded nothing!

What might be considered to be 'reasonable grounds for suspicion'?

☐ Does the suspicion have a sound foundation or is it just a 'gut feeling'?

☐ Ask yourself if another reasonable and honest person would have come to the same conclusion?

☐ If you made the decision not to report, would you be confident to defend that decision should there be an investigation in the future?

NB – The Data Protection Act gives an individual the right to access ALL information held on them. There must be no mention of 'Money Laundering' in your records. Suitable alternative phrases might be: 'Unusual Transactions', 'Satisfactory Explanation'. NEVER record anything that you do not want your client to read!

A report log must be kept; it must be separate from the client files, and notes must be kept only in the log to prevent 'Tipping Off' offences (see page 19).

So, what steps do you need to take?

- Decide which staff members will be responsible for submitting suspicion reports to your MLRO. Do they use own judgement or go through a supervisor?

- Decide on a process for reviewing transactions and arrangements, which are flagged up during ongoing monitoring, to decide grounds for suspicion.

- Set up formalised and secure methods by which staff can submit internally a suspicion report to MLRO and explain how the reports will be acknowledged and recorded.

- Write and circulate Policy & Procedure to all staff.

It is the responsibility of each staff member to submit a suspicion activity report directly to the MLRO, and you must hold a record of ALL suspicious activity reports made.

You are the MLRO and you receive an Internal Suspicion Report, what now?

When a report is received by the MLRO, they should:

- Check that the name, contact details, and signature of the reporting individual appear on the form
- The reason for the suspicion and any other relevant information
- Mark on the report, date & time received
- Give the report a unique, sequential identity number
- Acknowledge receipt of the report
- Check that ALL client due diligence documents are on file and accurate
- Begin enquiries – You MUST keep FULL records of any enquiries made, making contemporaneous notes, including deliberations and decisions – this all goes to demonstrate how effective your money laundering policy is and would also form your defence should you be accused of failings. You may need to ask the client questions, these questions MUST NOT arouse suspicion & all questions and responses must be recorded in writing

Things to consider during your enquiries:

1. Were all relevant identification checks carried out on the client?
2. Was a risk-based assessment completed?
3. When was the last review carried out?
4. Are the client's details still accurate?
5. Has the client appeared on a sanctions list or become a PEP?
6. If the client is a company, were ALL beneficial owners checked?
7. Was the client dormant and then suddenly became active again?
8. Has the client's investment strategy suddenly changed?
9. Has the frequency of transactions increased?
10. Has the type and/or size of investment suddenly changed?
11. If any changes have occurred, was a review or new due diligence carried out?

You do not have to link your suspicion to a particular deal or property, a suspicion of general criminal behaviour is all that is required.

Limits of any Enquiry

The enquiry is NOT a criminal investigation; when you submit a report to the NCA, they will decide if a full criminal investigation is necessary and will carry this out themselves. Your enquiries should be appropriate to the sector that you work in and corresponding client due diligence level; you are NOT looking for proof or corroborating facts, and it is certainly NOT your role to 'gather evidence' or interrogate suspects.

Possible outcomes from Internal Enquiry

1. ***No reasonable grounds to suspect Money Laundering*** – File the report – Include your findings and reasons for decision

2. ***There are reasonable grounds to suspect Money Laundering*** – Make a formal disclosure to the National Crime Agency (NCA), using either an 'online' or 'paper' submission. Give careful consideration to withdrawing from future business with the client. If business with your client is put on hold, you will be responsible for giving the affected staff consent to continue with the business in the future

3. ***Relationship frozen*** – Your MLRO is responsible for giving consent to reinstate business with the client

Formats for Internal Reports:

☐ Paper – This is the preferred format by authorities
☐ Email – Risk of breach of security

- Online Form – Suitable if you submit large numbers of reports
- Verbal – OK in an emergency, keep a record of the conversation and ask the staff member to submit a paper record immediately.

It is accepted that 'paper' reports are the best option taking into account security, best record format, and efficiency.

7) Disclosure to Authorities

Once you have decided that the level of suspicion or knowledge warrants reporting to the authorities, if this is your first report submission, then you must complete a Source Registrations Document, which is Appendix 1 of the SAR form.

There are several ways that your SAR report can be submitted:

Electronic

There are two methods of electronic submission:

- Via SAR Online – Web-based reporting – Most popular method (NCA website)

- Encrypted Bulk file submission – Larger organisations submitting large numbers

Paper

Not recommended by the NCA, but if unable to submit electronically, a form can be downloaded from the UK Financial Intelligence Unit (UKFIU). This must be printed, completed, and either faxed or posted to:

Post – UKFIU, PO Box 8000, London, SE11 5EN

Fax – 020 7238 8286

You must NOT scan completed document and email, as it will not be accepted.

Compulsory fields in the SAR report, which must be completed:

1. Reporting Institution
2. Your unique report log reference
3. Your branch or office
4. The disclosure date
5. The disclosure reason
6. The type – New or update
7. Client's surname or legal entity name

This is the minimum expected amount of information that will be accepted in a report.

Exceptions to the Duties to Report:

- The information came to you in privileged circumstances that is, in order for you to provide legal advice, such as explaining a client's tax liability, except when you judge that your advice has been sought to enable the client to commit a criminal offence or avoid detection, or expert opinion or services in relation to actual or contemplated legal proceedings.

- You have a reasonable excuse for not reporting, in which case you must report as soon as reasonable in the circumstances.

> **So, what steps do you need to take?**
>
> - Set up a process for the internal evaluation of the suspicion report and a routine for recording the process
>
> - Select a method for a formal disclosure to the authorities by submitting a Suspicious Activity Report (SAR) to the National Crime Agency (NCA) either ONLINE or PAPER
>
> - Register your company details with the NCA and prepare details needed for registration – So that you are ready to submit a SAR if you decide that a disclosure to the authorities is necessary at any stage
>
> - Circulate Policy & Procedure to ALL staff

If the subject of the suspicious report is on the 'Sanctions List', the MLRO MUST, regardless of the eventual decision, make a report to Her Majesty's Treasury (HMT) Sanctions & Illicit Finance Team – Email: financialsanctionshmtreasury.gsi.gov.uk

Once your report is received, if sent electronically you will receive acknowledgement of receipt, the information will be logged into the NCA database known as, ELMER. This information is then accessible to UK law enforcement bodies and other Government agencies.

Tipping off

If you know or suspect that a report has been made, you will commit an offence if you disclose any information that is likely to prejudice any actual or contemplated investigation following a report.

Note: The report does not have to have been made by you, you merely need to know or suspect that one has been made to an

MLRO, SOCA, HMRC or the police.

Freezing Transactions and Consent to Continue

If at the time of submitting your SAR to the NCA, you only 'suspect' criminal activity but you are already working with the client, and you feel that to suddenly terminate the relationship would raise suspicions and leave you open to a possible 'Tipping Off' offence, you can ask for permission to continue with the relationship during the initial assessment and any subsequent enquiry by the NCA themselves.

Reporters should also ensure the following when requesting consents to continue:

- Identify as clearly as possible the suspected benefit from criminal conduct including, where possible, the amount of benefit.

- Identify the reason for suspecting that property is criminal property.

- Identify the other party/parties involved in dealing with the criminal property including their dates of birth and addresses where available from CDD information.

You ask for permission to continue the relationship during the submission process for the SAR. There is a 'Consent Request' box to ✓ (appendix 2 of the SAR). When consent is given, this is known as 'Nominated Officer Consent'.

If you 'Know' that criminal activity has taken place, then you must 'freeze' the client's account and services that you were providing to them. If in doubt, ask for advice and guidance from the NCA team.

During this process, you MUST NOT TIP OFF the client.

You do not require consent when you:

- Do not intend to act in relation to the suspect property.

- Do intend to act, but you do not actually know or suspect that the property relates to money laundering or terrorist financing, even though reasonable grounds may exist.

Communication with Client while waiting for Consent

The reasons given below are acceptable to give to your client as explanations as to why the process has stopped following submission of your SAR to the NCA:

- Our systems are down

- I need the approval of a senior management member of staff, and they are away from the office

- We have new processes in the office, and the systems are running slow whilst bedding in.

Communication with client when withdrawing from the relationship

An acceptable reason:

- Compliance with Statutory Obligations

Refuse any further explanation

Complaints via your Ombudsman

During the decision-making time period by the NCA, a client may make a complaint to the ombudsman re the withdrawing of your services.

If approached by an ombudsman, you are permitted to disclose the real reason for the delay, e.g. SAR submitted to NCA. The ombudsman will liaise with the NCA and deal with the complaint appropriately going forward.

So, what steps do you need to take?

1. Put in place mechanism for stopping work and transactions of client affairs immediately an internal suspicion report is submitted ensuring that no business can go ahead without the express authority of the MLRO.

2. Set up formalised process for recording and tracking cases in which consent to continue is sought from the NCA when a formal disclosure has been made.

3. Establish a format for giving staff consent to continue with a client's business following a suspicion report, either on receipt of consent from the NCA or on the MLRO's authority.

4. Create a ready made procedure for communicating with clients who become aware that his/her business has been delayed, including some standard words that would avoid the risk of a 'tipping off' offence.

5. Send out Policy & Procedure to all staff.

Seller

The reasons for carrying out due diligence on the seller are two-fold, firstly, to prove that the person that you are dealing with is who they say they are, and secondly, that they have the right to sell or lease that property or site.

Seller Due Diligence Process

There are two ways to confirm the personal identity of your seller using photographic identification:

- Photo Driving Licence
- Current Passport.

As with the due diligence process for the investor, you **MUST** have seen the original document(s), obtain a copy, and hold on file. If you are away from your office, it is acceptable to use your phone or other device to take a clear image and save to the appropriate client file.

For a list of permitted documents, document formats, and those permitted to certify copies for UK and non-UK clients, please see chapter 7.

To confirm the current ownership of the property or site, you will need to download the 'Title Registration' from the Land Registry (12) site. The current charge per document downloaded is £3.00 per copy.

Property

I suppose it could be argued that the following requirements could be included as part of the vendor process, but as these are directly linked to a property, I have split the requirement out. So, what obligations might there be with regard to the property and legally being able to sell?

1) EPC certificate – It is a legal requirement that there is a current EPC certificate available to view or that at least all reasonable efforts have been made to do so within 7 days of first marketing the property. You can check to see if a property has a current certificate at the EPC Register site. (13)

2) Land Registry – Title Registration: Download and check the title registration; firstly, it should tell you when the property was purchased, and sometimes it states the purchase price. Whether the property is 'leasehold' or 'freehold', it may also confirm the owners' name and their address at the time of purchase; as well as stating if there are any 'legal charges' (12) against the property; usually from a mortgage provider and also known as a 'first charge'.

3) Land Registry – Although not a legal requirement, we as a matter of course download and check the 'Title Plan' to ensure that the site boundary is the same as stated by the vendor and our visible checks when the property is viewed.

Not only is the EPC certificate a lawful requirement, but since the implementation of the 4th Money Laundering Directive, which made it a lawful requirement for estate agents to carry out due diligence not only on their clients, the seller but also the buyer as well – we as property sourcers must not only carry out due diligence on our clients the buyers but also the vendor and property.

If you are sourcing through an estate agent, then maybe we should be asking questions as to whether the full due diligence process has been carried out.

To ensure that any deals we send to our clients are fully checked, as a matter of course we download the title registration and plan as these can act as a great source of information to help confirm that the person claiming to be the vendor actually is who they say they are.

There have been several cases where professionals have failed to do this with serious consequences; one such example is described below:

The case of Purrunsing v A'Court & Co (ACC) and Anor (2016) (14) was brought to court by the buyer of a property in Wimbledon who was subsequently awarded damages of £470,000 for his loss in the case.

The case came about when Mr Purrunsing purchased a property in Wimbledon, from Mr Dawson who claimed to be the legal owner but who turned out to be a fraudster and had no legal right to sell the property. The purchase price of the property was £470,000, and the whole payment was made to a bank in Dubai, where the seller claimed that he now lived and needed a quick sale. By the time it was realised that there had been a case of fraud, the money had been lost and was never recovered.

The judge found that no serious attempt had been made to carry out a risk-based assessment of the sale and comply with anti-money laundering regulations. No one had obtained documentation linking the seller with the property, and no checks were made with any addresses provided by the seller.

In this case, it was the solicitor and a conveyancer that had to pay the damages awarded. How long will it be before we as property sourcers are in the spotlight because we didn't carry out due diligence checks on our sellers or buyers'?

Could you afford to pay damages up to the full value paid for a property that you have sourced; I somehow doubt it!

The old adage of 'Buyer Beware' is no substitute for compliance with the requirements of the money laundering regulations.

Key points to take away

Sourcing Agents:

1. Ensure that you have a due diligence process in place for the seller, property and investor.

2. Keep the processes simple, for example for the investor consider keeping to a two level CDD.

3. Make sure that you record everything, keep full and accurate records.

4. Do not jump steps in the CDD process just to get some fees in the bank.

5. Have a staff training record and programme in place and stick to it.

6. If you cannot complete a CDD process, do not enter into a business relationship with that person, whether that is a seller or an investor.

Investors:

1. It is the responsibility of the property sourcer to carry out due diligence on you, your company and your funds. The process can appear to be intrusive, but if it is carried out with a professional, adaptive approach it does not have to be onerous.

2. Ask the property sourcer what their due diligence process consists of, can they explain what the steps of their process are and an approximate time span for completion?

3. Is their process adaptable to your required pace?

4. What due diligence process do they carry out on the seller and the property?

Chapter 7 – Optional Professional Registrations

Residential Landlords Association (RLA)

The RLA was the first national landlords association and at this time represents over 22,000 landlords with combined portfolio in excess of £250 million. They are there to support their members with an advisory service with regard to anything pertinent to the rental sector, tenants, and landlord responsibilities.

Regulatory Requirements:

To become a member, you <u>do not</u> have to prove membership of any other professional bodies including redress schemes, data protection, or anti-money laundering.

Codes of Conduct Required:

The code of conduct and disciplinary procedures are binding on all members. There are two sections to this:

1. Code of Conduct – This has 16 Rules ranging from complying with legal obligations to conflicts of interest & confidentiality

2. Disciplinary – This has a five-step process, is an integral part of the codes of practice and will be observed by all members.

Cost of membership:

There are two levels of membership:

1. Landlord Membership - £79.95 per year (Direct Debit)
2. Corporate Membership - £154.95 per year (Direct Debit)

Their website has lots of information, documents, and contracts which members can download and use. They have other services available such as landlord insurance and Deposit Guard.

National Federation of Property Professionals (NFoPP) – Since March 2017 known as 'Propertymark'

The NFoPP was formed in 2007 as a result of renaming The National Association of Estate Agents. They state that their aim is to '... promote the highest standards of professionalism and integrity among those working within the property industry...' Running in excess of 250 short courses each year covering a variety of subjects linked to the property sector. In March 2017, the NFoPP became Propertymark; the change was instigated as it was felt that even professionals within the industry did not relate to it, and it was, therefore, time for change. Propertymark is now the named provider for all courses as well as being the overall responsible body for the following associations:

- National Association of Estate Agents (NAEA)

- Association of Residential Lettings Agents (ARLA)

- Institution of Commercial and Business Agents (ICBA)

- National Association of Valuers and Auctioneers (NAVA)

- Association of Professional Inventory Providers (APIP)

You cannot become a member of the NFoPP (Propertymark) only one of their associates such as the NAEA. Upon joining, you must agree to comply with the professional standards set within the Propertymark Code of Conduct and membership rules. This is the same for any of the above linked associations.

National Association of Estate Agents (NAEA)

Members join the NAEA voluntarily, their clients can be reassured that all members are compliant with current regulations and operate to a high level of integrity.

Regulatory Requirements: – Redress Scheme, PI Insurance, Anti-Money Laundering, Data Protection, client account reporting, and client money protection.

Codes of Conduct Required: Propertymark

Cost of membership:

Student Grade – This grade is open to anyone; you do not have to be working in the industry or have any qualifications. However, it is not open to Principles, Partners, or Directors (PPD's) of property related companies. This is purely a route into membership whilst studying for the relevant qualification with the support of the NAEA.

Time Allowance – 3 Years

Fee: Annual Subscription - £90.00 + One off application fee - £50.00

You also get a £100.00 study material discount.

Associate Grade (ANAEA)- Must be working as a residential estate agent and have at least five years experience as a residential sales agent. You do not need any formal qualifications for this membership level. However, during the application process, you will be asked to provide your CV detailing experience as well as providing references.

If you are a PPD, then there are extra obligations to adhere to and prove continuing compliance annually through attendance of official conferences, meetings, or training programmes run by Propertymark.

Annual Continuing Professional Development (CPD) – 12 hours

Fee: Annual Subscription - £230.00 + One off application fee - £50.00

Member Grade (MNAEA) – Must be working for a residential estate agency and must hold a Level 3 Technical Ward in Sale of Residential Property or a comparable accepted by the Association.

If you are a PPD, then there are extra obligations to adhere to and prove continuing compliance annually through attendance of official conferences, meetings, or training programmes run by the NFoPP.

Annual Continuing Professional Development (CPD) – 12 hours

Fee: Annual Subscription - £230.00 + One off application fee - £50.00

Fellow Grade (FNAEA) – Must be working as a residential sales agent, have at least five years experience and also have a relevant qualification (Level 4 Certificate in Sale of Residential Property) or a comparable accepted by the Association.

Again, if you are a PPD, then there are extra obligations to adhere to and prove continuing compliance annually through attendance of official conferences, meetings or training programmes run by the NFoPP.

Annual Continuing Professional Development (CPD) – 12 hours

Fee: Annual Subscription - £230.00 + One off application fee - £50.00

1. You must be a member of a government approved redress scheme – See Chapter 3 for details on the schemes available.

2. You must have Professional Indemnity Insurance – Annual income up to £150k must have minimum £150k cover – Over £150k income must have minimum £500k – The cover must be on a civil liability basis, the limit must be on an "any one claim" basis, indemnity to include any claim arising out of all work undertaken since inception of the business and cover for liability arising out of all aspects of the PPD member firms activities.

3. Client Account reporting – If your company handles client monies, then a Propertymark accountant's report must be submitted annually within six months of the company's financial year end.

4. Client Money Protection (CMP) – A scheme of compensation run by the NFoPP for landlords, tenants, and other clients should an agent misappropriate their rent, deposit, or other client funds.

5. Registered for Anti-Money Laundering supervision (HMRC) see chapter 3

6. Registered for Data Protection (ICO) see Chapter 3.

Association of Residential Letting Agents (ARLA)

ARLA is the UK's foremost professional body for Letting Agents. All members must maintain the highest of professional standards providing clients with peace of mind that they will receive a high standard of service or should things go wrong have a professional service that they can approach for support and help.

If you are a PPD, then there are extra obligations to adhere to and prove continuing compliance annually through attendance of official conferences, meetings or training programmes run by the NFoPP, a minimum of 12 hours Continuing Professional Development (CPD) annually.

Regulatory Requirements: PI Insurance, Client Money Protection (CMP)

Codes of Conduct Required: Propertymark

Cost of membership:

There are two membership grades:

Member Grade (MARLA): Must be working in the residential letting sector for an ARLA licenced company and have a Level 2-3 Technical Award in Residential Lettings and Property Management, or a comparable qualification accepted by the Association.

Annual Continuing Professional Development (CPD) – 12 hours

Fee: Annual Subscription - £225.00 + One off application fee - £50.00

Fellow Grade (FARLA): Must be working in the residential letting sector, have a minimum of five years experience and have a Level 4 Technical Award in Residential Lettings and Property Management, or a comparable qualification accepted by the Association.

Annual Continuing Professional Development (CPD) – 12 hours

Fee: Annual Subscription - £225.00 + One off application fee - £50.00

National Association of Property Buyers (NAPB)

The NAPB was formed by a group of property professionals in 2013 and has since worked closely with The Property Ombudsman to help form codes of practice that could aid the raising of standards across the industry. There are currently 28 members registered.

Regulatory Requirements: PI Insurance, Client Money Protection, Member TPO

Codes of Conduct Required: TPO

You have to complete an application form and return by either post or email.

<u>Membership</u>: You must be a company that purchases properties directly from the homeowner, be a member of The Property Ombudsman Scheme for Residential Property Buying Companies and have PI Insurance that specifies 'Property Buying Services'.

Fee: Annual Subscription - £200.00

National Crime Agency (NCA)

The NCA's role is to protect the public from serious threats and bring to justice those serious and organised criminals who pose the highest risk to the UK. In 2015, they formed the Joint Money Laundering Task Force in partnership with the financial sector to target criminal gangs carrying out 'high end' money laundering crimes.

Should you suspect a client of money laundering, you must submit a Suspicious Activity Report (SAR) to the NCA and to make the submission you need to register with them (you do not need to register until you need to make a submission to them).

Regulatory Requirements: To submit a SAR's report when you suspect that money laundering has or may be committed by your client.

Codes of Conduct Required: Must submit SAR's reports through the NCA (more detail in Client Due Diligence Chapter 4)

Fee: No Registration Fee

Key points to take away

Sourcing Agents:

1. Whilst all of these bodies are an option for you to join and not compulsory, having their logo on your website, social media and documentation adds an element of trust for your potential clients.

2. From a purely business aspect, being a member of these associations also opens doors to a network of expertise and support that may be difficult to access elsewhere; including quite often legal advice.

Investors:

1. If your chosen sourcer is a member of any of the above associations, it might reflect their intentions of working to the highest standards to provide you with the best possible service.

2. Always check that your sourcer actually is registered with any professional body, don't just take it as a given!

Chapter 8 – I am Insured and Registered – What now?

You are registered with a Property Redress Scheme, Data Protection, Anti-Money Laundering and obtained Professional Indemnity Insurance. You have a reasonable knowledge of what legislation and regulation your business is governed by, and your company terms and conditions along with contracts are in place, "That is it, right?" Well, actually that is just the beginning; now you have to comply with those regulations, membership rules, and guidelines every day, day in day out; so how do you do that?

There are some ongoing systems, which can be implemented and used to maintain, improve, monitor, and not only ensure compliance but also aid the successful development of any business. These systems although independent of each other, when brought together and set up from the start can transform your business, allowing you to expand, easily outsourcing some tasks without losing control over the quality of service provided. So, what are these systems that you need to implement sooner rather than later:

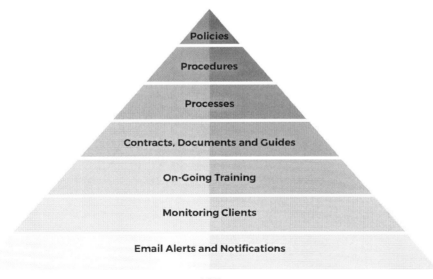

I know that most of you are now asking yourself, "Do I really need all of these now?" "Is there really a difference between policies, processes, and procedures; aren't they all the same?"

Well, the vast majority of businesses make the mistake of only having one or two of these systems in place when all are essential; so what does each system cover:

- Policies – These are the guidelines, rules or laws of your company.

- Procedures – These are the clearly defined steps required to adhere to any policy.

- Processes – These are the step-by-step actions that need to be taken to fulfil a specific procedure.

- Contracts – Such as business terms and conditions, option agreement, and sole agency agreement, etc.

- Documents – Such as response letters for complaints, etc.

- Guides – Such as a 'company introduction' sheet as to what your company does, In-House complaints process, information about EPC's, etc.

- Ongoing Training – Ensure that you and your staff have received and have logged any necessary training.

- Email Alerts & Notifications – Many professional registration bodies offer you the ability to sign up for email alerts or notifications for any changes to regulations, codes of practice, or just something of interest to your sector.

- Ongoing monitoring of existing clients (investors) and their transactions.

Let's have a look at each of these groups in turn:

1. Policies, Procedures, and Processes

Going forward, you will need the following in place as a minimum. Should you be inspected, you need to show that you not only have these policies and procedures in place, you also need to show you have processes to back them up so that it helps you to prove you not only understand your obligations but that you also work to high standards of compliance every day.

> *Here is an example to help you understand the difference between them: You receive a complaint in writing from a client: a) Policy: states that you will acknowledge receipt of the complaint within three working days, b) Procedure: states that to respond to the initial complaint, you use the 'Initial Response Letter', c) Process: gives detailed instructions as to where to find the letter, how to complete/fill in the blanks and how to send to the client.*

Remember that some professional registrations make having them part of your code of compliance for that membership, so please make sure that you know which these are. I have listed the ones that we use below in more detail; each sub-category is a policy, procedure, and quite often a process in itself:

a) Anti-Money Laundering:

    i.   Assessment of Money Laundering Risk
    ii.   Verification of ID
    iii.   Knowing Your Clients
    iv.   Ongoing Monitoring
    v.   Record Keeping
    vi.   Internal Suspicion Report
    vii.   Disclosure to Authorities
    viii.   Freezing Transactions & Consent to Continue
    ix.   Training
    x.   Monitoring & Management of Compliance

b) Anti-Bribery:

     i.   Bribery Prevention
    ii.   Commissions
   iii.   Business Gifts – Offering
   iv.   Business Gifts – Accepting
    v.   Offering and accepting hospitality, entertainment or similar
   vi.   Accepting or offering travel and accommodation costs
  vii.   Appointing staff and outside persons or organisations
 viii.   Training and communication
   ix.   Monitoring and review

c) Anti-Fraud

d) Data Protection

e) Internal Complaints Handling

2. Contracts, Documents, and Guides

Whilst this is covered in greater detail in Chapter 5, here are the basic requirements again:

☐ General – Seller & Investor guides giving information about your company, the services that you provide, and how that will work. Examples of previous deals (investors) and details about your professional registrations and why they are so important (this may well set you apart from your competitors).

☐ Seller – Personal Data Capture Form, Sole Agency Agreement or Option agreement, Misdescription Form.

☐ Investor - Data Capture Form, Investment Pro Forma, Business Terms and Conditions and Sourcing Fee Agreement/Deal Introduction Form.

3. Ongoing Training

Training can be carried out 'in-house', or there are many online training companies that provide niche training, such as anti-money laundering, bribery, and fraud or data protection. Ensure that all new staff members receive a rigorous training programme as part of their induction into your company. Both you and your staff should also receive at least annual refresher training to refresh knowledge and also address any updates in legislation, regulation, or required codes of practice.

Make your training relevant to your sector, giving scenarios for each subject being taught. This may enhance the overall learning experience, helping to explain situations that your staff may come across on a day-to-day basis and provide them with the ability to be able to confidently deal with their individual roles.

You must make sure that you have a system (simple training spreadsheet is provided in your free download package) in place to record training data; it must be in use and effective:

☐ Show staff name, job role, and which courses are relevant to each staff member, e.g. money laundering, data protection, etc.

☐ Show the date that each staff member received the training in each subject and at what level, e.g. Induction or refresher.

☐ A record of whether a post training competence test was carried out.

☐ Show a date for when next training is due.

Here are specific requirements for some of the regulations:

Money Laundering

As a property sourcing business, some of your staff but not all, may have contact with clients on a regular basis. It is recommended that at the very least your relevant staff should be aware of the following:

- What the underlying purpose is behind money laundering and whether something may be the proceeds of crime or terrorist related.

- The criminal offence(s) related to money laundering.

- The Money Laundering Regulations.

- Their personal obligations under the legislation and regulation.

- Your companies AML policies, processes, and procedures (confirmation of identification, client due diligence, record keeping and suspicion reporting).

- Examples of how suspicions might be raised in your sector.

- The identity of your companies Money Laundering Reporting Officer (MLRO) and any process for submitting an 'Internal Suspicion Report'.

Guides:

- An information sheet or guide for staff that informs them of their personal obligations with regard to money laundering prevention which must be made available to all relevant staff at all times.

The law does not specify at what intervals training should be provided; but HMRC stipulate that staff should receive training if new to your company, through a change in job role and should as a matter of course receive training at least every two years.

Data Protection

As stated earlier in the chapter, you do not have to carry out training in-house, you could outsource your training to an online training company. There are some things that you should include in your data protection training and ensure that your staff understand the following:

☐ How to keep passwords secure?

☐ To secure computers when not in use.

☐ To dispose of confidential documents securely.

☐ To take care when visiting unknown websites and opening emails – Virus attacks.

☐ To ensure that their desk is clear of sensitive personal information.

☐ To keep secure backups for information.

☐ Any visitors are signed in and out and accompanied at all times.

☐ To ensure that they have permission to share personal information.

☐ How to deal with a request for a copy of personal information held?

☐ That as a company you have up to 40 days to respond to a request for information held.

☐ That the maximum fee that can be charged to provide that information is £10.

☐ That they need to check the identification of the person asking for the information.

The law does not specify at what intervals training should be provided, but staff should receive training if new to your company, have a change in job role and should as a matter of course receive refresher training at least every two years or to cover any changes in regulations or professional guidance.

Bribery

As with the other subjects covered above, it is wise to make training mandatory for all new staff and carry out refresher courses either at two-year intervals or as required by changes in regulations, etc. Again, adapt the training to individual members of staff dependent on their job role, and as always use scenarios to make it easier for them to understand the point that you are trying to get over based on their day-to-day work processes.

Fraud

The same as bribery above, it is wise to make training mandatory for all new staff and carry out refresher courses as required. Adapt the training to individual members of staff dependent on their job role and use scenarios to make it easier for them to understand the point that you are trying to get over based on their day-to-day work processes.

4. Email Alerts, Newsletters & Notifications

You will need to monitor for changes to Legislation, Regulation, Professional Registration rules, and industry news in general. There are several sites listed under the group: Email Alerts, Newsletters, and Notifications in the 'Resources' page at the back of this book, also available as a free download.

5. Ongoing Monitoring of Existing Clients (Investors) and their Transactions

You must apply ongoing monitoring to existing clients. This means that you must:

- Carry out appropriate and risk-sensitive CDD measures to any transaction, which appears to be inconsistent with your knowledge of the client, or the client's business, or risk profile. For example, if a client suddenly has an injection of significant funds, check the source of funds. If a beneficial owner is revealed, obtain evidence of the beneficial owner's identity and the nature and purpose of the injection of the funds.

- Keep CDD documents, data and information up to date; for example, if a client company has a change to its directorship, update your records accordingly.

Questions to Ask:

- Ask yourself, if the client came to you as a new client today, would the information that you currently have be sufficient or do you require more?

- Apply risk sensitive CDD measures to each transaction carried out – For example, is this transaction out of character with their other transactions? Have they suddenly had an injection of large sums of money? – Check the source of the funds – If beneficial owner of funds found, evidence identity and look into purpose of funds injection.

- Regularly update your details held including changes of address, formation of companies, changes to directors or shareholders, etc.

6. Packaging and Marketing Deals

a) Simple Brokering

There are some things to consider when packaging and marketing your deals. The Financial Conduct Authority (FCA) does not regulate property sourcers as they are classified as estate agents who simply broker deals. That means that they link a seller/property and a buyer together and upon exchange of contracts receive a fee for that service. If you follow this format of packaging and marketing, then you can promote your deal to anyone.

You can include in your marketing such things as:

- Purchase cost.

- Potential rental income achievable – You could reference the Local Housing Allowance (LHA) rates or current, comparable data from Rightmove or Zoopla.

- Return on Investment (ROI) – as long as you use a straightforward calculation, which is based on known, provable figures, and the formulae used is declared and clear.

- Illustrate possible finance options – Do not state whether you consider them to be good or bad as this could be considered to be examples of personal opinion or providing financial advice.

Whatever figures you use, it is important that you can prove them, so whether you use LHA, Rightmove, or Zoopla for your comparable data, whilst not explicitly required, it might be considered best practice to take screenshots of the figures found and provide them in your presentation.

You can fall foul of the law by breaching the FCA's digital advertising guidelines. As an estate agent or property sourcer, you are not qualified to provide financial advice, and it would be wise to avoid offering personal opinions or advice as to the quality of an investment opportunity. If you were to use any of the following terms (this is by no means a definitive list) as well as a 'call to action', you may be in breach of the guidance:

- Investment Deal
- Investment Opportunity
- Return
- Performance
- Gains
- Guaranteed

For example, the headline for your current deal for which you are direct to seller and looking for a single buyer:

'Great Investment Opportunity, 30% Return on your Cash Invested' – contact me at abc@123.com for more details.

As an agent or property sourcer, anyone of legal age can buy the deal from you; the potential issue with any advertisement is around whether it is fair and accurate, that it does not express whether the investment is good or bad and does not make suggestions about returns that you cannot back up with facts. In short, it is advisable not to tell people what to think, but present provable facts and let the potential buyer form their own opinions as to whether it is right for them or not.

If however, the above advertisement were being used to attract a joint venture partner, a cash investor or a small group of people to team up with, you are no longer brokering the deal, you would be looking for JV partners, and this triggers a completely different set of issues.

b) JV's & Profit Sharing

The FCA regulates the promotion of financial investment but is generally not interested in 'loans', as long as you are the one doing the borrowing. Those individuals who are authorised by the FCA can promote financial investment opportunities within the guidelines. If you are not approved by the FCA for financial promotions, then assume that it would be illegal for you to do so. There are, however, some exceptions which we will cover in more detail later in this section.

If any deal that you promote provides a way for an investor to make a financial return, then it is a 'financial promotion' in the broadest sense of the term, whether that deal is for buy to let, rent-to-rent, serviced accommodation, residential or commercial developments or any other type of investment strategy. If you are an agent simply brokering or selling the deal on, then you would probably be fine; if, however, you are remaining in the project, then you need to seek legal advice before taking any steps to advertise or seek out JV partners. The crime committed is never in doing the deal, but in sharing the information.

The FCA does however, focus heavily on financial opportunity promotion, and Section 21 of the regulations prevents promotion of an Unregulated Collective Investment Scheme (UCIS) to the general public. The legal framework for this came into force in 2003, but it was not until 2014 that the FCA published their policy statement 13/3, more commonly known as PS13/3.

This policy becomes relevant when you want to attract capital for a deal within the format of a JV, which would be considered to be a UCIS.

You are engaged in investment activity if you are communicating via:

- Face to face

- Phone call
- Email
- Advertisements
- Website
- Presentation

Exemptions from the regulations are:

- Existing shareholders
- Family members
- Long-standing friends

Many of you will already be familiar with the terms 'high net worth' and 'sophisticated investor'. If you are advertising a deal to attract JV partners, you do not have to be 'high net worth' nor a 'sophisticated investor', but your JV partner(s) do.

There is of course still the problem that you are not allowed to share any details of your project with people who are not exempt, that is neither 'high net worth' nor 'sophisticated investors'. You must, therefore, only communicate or provide details of your project to those people that you have already gathered evidence to prove their status as to exemption.

If you still wish to deal with potential JV partners directly, there are two more obligations to fulfil even after you have proved that they are exempt. The legislation imposes a duty of care upon the party who is looking to raise the funds from others to complete the project, and they must show that:

1. The investor(s) clearly understand the investment and any associated risks?
2. That the investment is suitable for that person at this time?

Please educate yourself with regard to these regulations and be aware as to how your presentations are structured and marketed, as penalties for breaching these regulations could be very painful, with heavy fines, liquidation of the investment or imprisonment being within the FCA's powers.

If you promote your deals in this way, you must consider any of your investors as restricted until you prove that they are exempt, if they are in one of the two categories described above. You must also maintain accurate, up to date records on your investors as the FCA may request to see them.

You must obtain evidence to prove the status of your investors; see some examples below:

<u>High Net Worth</u>

- £100,000 income – Obtain a copy of the previous year's P60 and also copies of all pay slips for the current year to show that the level of income is still current or the investor may be able to provide documentation from his accountant to prove income.

- Investable assets greater than £250,000 – Use your personal data capture form to ask the investor to list all properties, sites, and other investments currently owned (excluding primary residence, value of their pensions or any 'live' insurance policies) with an overall current value. Obtain copies of title registers for any properties listed to prove ownership and for other investments obtain confirmation from the investor's accountant as to existence and current value.

<u>Sophisticated Investor</u>

The FCA definition for a sophisticated investor states that they are retail clients with extensive investment experience and knowledge of complex instruments who are better able to understand the risk. The FCA also stipulate specific categories by which someone would be judged as being a 'sophisticated investor':

- Having had more than one direct investment in an unlisted company in the last 12 months – An example of proof would be a screenshot of two equity investments on an FCA regulated crowd-funding site.

- A member of a network or syndicate of business angels – this would not include a monthly property investors' meet, but more along the lines of a well-recognised group such as the British Venture Capital Association.

- Anyone that is working or has worked in the last two years in the private equity sector or the provision of finance to SME's is considered 'sophisticated'.

- Has been a director of a company within the last two years where the company has a £1 million or greater turnover.

When dealing with exempt individuals, you will need to prove the exemption by obtaining evidence to verify their status before communicating or providing any information about the project; do not just accept the investors' word.

Individuals are allowed to self-certify that they qualify as a high net worth or sophisticated investor. It might be considered best practice to allow the individual to sign a self-certification declaration and then ask for the supporting evidence for the category the investor has indicated they qualify for.

You must believe that the self-certification is valid rather than simply blindly accepting a signed self-certification form at face value. The risk is that you may well have failed to meet good standards in your due diligence process.

Even if the investor was exempt in the past, you still need to re-run the checks each year. If they subsequently fail to qualify, you MUST manage them out of the investment with no harm to them. The removal is compulsory; they cannot 'vote' to remain in the investment.

If you are brokering the deal as an estate agent or property sourcer, you are more likely to be fine; if you are intending to remain in the deal in some way, then you need to seek legal advice before proceeding.

Please educate yourself with regard to these regulations and be aware as to how your presentations are structured and marketed, as penalties for breaches of FCA guidelines could be very painful. In 2016, fines issued across all FCA guidelines ranged from £17,900 to £8,246,800. (1)

Key points to take away

Sourcing Agents:

1. You will need to have certain policies, procedures and processes in place.

2. You will also need certain guides, letters, documents, agreements and contracts created and preferably checked by an experienced commercial contracts solicitor.

3. You will need an in-house training programme.

4. Have a process, which allows you to stay up to date with changes in legislation or regulation from email alerts, newsletters or notifications.

5. Have a system in place for monitoring your clients and transactions.

6. Be aware of the restrictions on how you can package a deal if you want to market to the general public.

Investors:

1. Does the agent have any policies and procedure, such as data protection and money laundering?

2. Do their documents, agreements and contracts appear professional, clear and fair?

3. How are their deals packaged and presented, are they sending you deals that fulfil your requirements or are they sending you everything and the 'kitchen sink'?

4. Do they understand their responsibilities with regard to key areas such as data protection and money laundering?

5. If you have any doubts, may be you should consider finding another sourcing agent to work with.

Final Thoughts

My original notes for this page, written some time ago, had the opening sentence as ...

"I hope that you enjoyed reading my book..."

When I read this recently, I chuckled to myself because I realise that for most of you, the words legislation, regulation, and compliance definitely do not go hand in hand with enjoyment!

So I will instead say ...

"I hope that you found my book to be informative"

I would just like to add that whilst the information in this book is a great starting point, a reference guide that you can refer back to time and time again, it is not the 'be all and end all' of the subject. I urge you, whether you are an investor or a sourcer, to carry on reading and learning. One of the smartest areas to invest in is your own education.

It would be a pleasure to meet you in person at one of my live events and hear about your journey or maybe help you further with an online course. In the meantime, I wish you every success with either your property sourcing business or your investments in the property sector.

Tina

References

Introduction

(1) 'National Strategic Assessment of Serious and Organised Crime 2016', NCA, September 2016

(2) http://www.rossmartin.co.uk/sme-tax-news/2358-hmrc-fine-for-anti-money-laundering-failures

Chapter 1

(1) 'Money Laundering Regulations 2007: Supervision of Estate Agency Business

Chapter 2

(1) IT Governance - https://www.itgovernance.co.uk/dpa-penalties

Chapter 3

(1) National Trading Standards Estate Agency Team Powys - http://www.powys.gov.uk/en/licensing-trading-standards/national-estate-agency-standards/advice-for-estate-agents/

(2) FCA 2016 Fines Issued - https://www.fca.org.uk/news/news-stories/2016-fines

Chapter 4

(1) Property Industry Eye - http://www.propertyindustryeye.com/letting-agent-fined-after-not-joining-redress-scheme/

(2) Ardrossan Harold – http://www.ardrossanherald.com/news/14101398.Darlington_letting_agents_fined_after_council_investigation/

(3) Letting Agent Today -
https://www.lettingagenttoday.co.uk/breaking-news/2015/7/11-
agents-fined-37k-for-not-joiningredressschemes

(4) The Property Ombudsman - https://www.tpos.co.uk/news-media-
and-press-releases/case-studies/item/gentle-pressure-and-
questionable-offers

(5) The Property Redress Scheme -
https://www.theprs.co.uk/Resource/ViewFile/121

(6) Ombudsman Services - https://www.ombudsman-
services.org/downloads/Anoncasesummaries_property.pdf

(7) The National Crime Agency -
http://www.nationalcrimeagency.gov.uk/publications/731-national-
strategic-assessment-of-serious-and-organised-crime-2016/file

(8) Open Government -
http://www.opengovernment.org.uk/resource/ogn-submission-make-
company-ownership-transparent/

(9) The National Crime Agency -
http://www.nationalcrimeagency.gov.uk/publications/677-sars-annual-
report-2015/file

(10) Money Laundering Compliance -
http://www.moneylaunderingcompliance.com/index.php/general-
information/money-laundering-supervison

(11) Information Commissioners Office -
https://ico.org.uk/actionwevetaken/enforcement/?facet_type=Prosecuti
ons&facet_sector=&facet_date=&date_from=&date_to=

Chapter 6

(1) Financial Action Task Force (FATF) Guide – Search for PEP's
(Recommendations 12 & 22) - http://bit.ly/1sNFNi0

(2) Government Guides: People of Significant Control -

http://bit.ly/1Tuq6bL

(3) Companies House: Company search - http://bit.ly/1IwqDzD

(4) GoBanking Rates: 12 Best Tax Havens - http://bit.ly/2reyB2z

(5) Land Registry: Overseas Ownership - http://bit.ly/1R0eknD

(6) Pan-European Beneficial Ownership Register – Expected soon - http://bit.ly/2qypnKK

(7) Government Overseas Companies Data - http://bit.ly/29aSrAb

(8) Joint Money Laundering Steering Group (JMLSG) Introduction Forms Templates - http://jmlsg.org.uk/download/5053

(9) Government Consolidated Sanctions List - http://bit.ly/1jFLBSj

(10) SAR Submitting - http://bit.ly/2quySv5

(11) NCA – www.nationalcrimeagency.gov.uk

(12) Land Registry - http://bit.ly/2rxsOWM

(13) EPC Register - http://bit.ly/1mNfW1k

(14) Legal Futures Report - http://bit.ly/2rfKRA2

Chapter 8

(1) FCA Fines 2016 - http://bit.ly/2gWmGiS

Glossary of Terms

AML – Anti-Money Laundering

AMLL – Anti-Money Laundering Legislation

APIP – Association of Professional Inventory Providers

AR – Annual Return

ARLA – Association of Residential Letting Agents

B of E – Bank of England

BIS – Department for Business Innovation and Skills

BPR's – The Business Protection from Misleading Marketing Regulations 2008

BTL – Buy to Let

CDD – Client Due Diligence

CEARA – The Consumers, Estate Agents and Redress Act 2007

CMP – Client Money Protection

CPD - Continuing Professional Development

CPR's – The Consumer Protection from Unfair Trading Regulations 2008

CRM – Customer Relationship Management

DD – Due Diligence

DP – Data Protection

D & O – Director and Officer's (Insurance)

EDD – Enhanced Due Diligence

EEA – European Economic Area

EMC's – Enhanced Consumer Measures

EPC – Energy Performance Certificate

EU – European Union

FATF – Financial Action Task Force

FCA – Financial Conduct Authority

GDPR – The General Data Protection Regulations 2016

HMO – House of Multiple Occupation

HMRC – Her Majesty's Revenue and Customs

HMT – Her Majesty's Treasury

HSE – The Health and Safety Executive

ICBA – Institution of Commercial and Business Agents

ICO – Information Commissioners Office

IMF – International Monetary Fund

Investor – Buyer

ID - Identification

IoAC – Isle of Anglesey Council

IP – Income Protection (Insurance)

JMLSG – Joint Money Laundering Steering Group

LA – Local Authority

LHA – Local Housing Allowance

Lien – A right to hold property belonging to another person until a debt owed by that person has been discharged

LLP – Limited Liability Partnership

MD – Managing Director

ML – Money Laundering

MLR – Money Laundering Regulations 2007

MLRO – Money Laundering Responsible Officer

NAEA – National Association of Estate Agents

NALS – National Approved Letting Scheme

NAPB – National Association of Property Buyers

NAVA – National Association of Valuers and Auctioneers

NCA – National Crime Agency

NFoPP – National Federation of Property Professionals

NTSEAT – National Trading Standards Estate Agency Team

NW – North West

OA – Option Agreement

OFT – Office of Fair Trade

PCC – Powys County Council

PCN – Penalty Charge Notice

PEP – Politically Exposed Person

PI – Professional Indemnity (Insurance)

PL – Public Liability (Insurance)

PoCA – The Proceeds of Crime Act 2002

PRS – Property Redress Scheme

PSC – People with Significant Control

RLA – Residential Landlords Association

RICS – Royal Institute of Chartered Surveyors

ROI – Return on Investment

SA – Serviced Accommodation

SAR – Suspicious Activity Report

SDD – Standard Due Diligence

SOCA – Serious Organised Crime Agency

TA – The Terrorism Act 2000

T's & C's – Terms and Conditions

TPO – The Property Ombudsman

UK – United Kingdom

UKALA – UK Association of Letting Agents

UKFIU – UK Financial Intelligence Unit

VAT – Value Added Tax

Vendor – Property or site owner (Seller)

Resources

Legislation:

- **The Estate Agents Act 1979** - http://bit.ly/2l7lptG

- **The Consumers, Estate Agents and Redress Act 2007** - http://bit.ly/2kmgTYX

- **The Data Protection Act 1998** - http://bit.ly/18Er0gh

- **The Proceeds of Crime Act 2002** - http://bit.ly/1fF1Mhp

- **The Terrorism Act 2000** - http://bit.ly/2dIBH8l

- **The Bribery Act 2010** - http://bit.ly/1FIc0c7

- **The Consumer Rights Act 2015** - http://bit.ly/19Aujpw

- **The Enterprise Act 2002** – http://bit.ly/2n3q14T

- **The Financial Services and Markets Act 2000 (FSMA) as updated by the Financial Services Act 2012** - http://bit.ly/2dKLXLP

Regulations:

- **Money Laundering Regulations 2007** - http://bit.ly/2kFJ9ll

- **The Consumer Contracts (Information, Cancellation and Additional Charges) Regulations 2013 (CCRs)** - http://bit.ly/1i0TDZi

- **The Consumer Protection from Unfair Trading Regulations 2008** - http://bit.ly/19kAFtA

- **The Business Protection from Misleading Marketing Regulations (October 2008) BPR's** – http://bit.ly/2qO3abr

- **The Electronic Commerce (EC Directive) Regulations 2002** - http://bit.ly/2mTrzyz

- **Provision of Services Regulations 2009** - http://bit.ly/2nPTKeF

- **The Energy Performance of Buildings (England and Wales) (Amendment) Regulations 2014** - http://bit.ly/1nb9cMh

- **The Town and Country Planning (Control of Advertisements) Regulations** - http://bit.ly/2mzgI8E

- **The Estate Agents (Accounts) Regulations 1981** - http://bit.ly/2qIYA2Z

- **The Companies Act 2006, and the Companies, LLP and Business (Names and Trading Disclosures) Regulations 2015** - http://bit.ly/1BXkaOt

Property Redress Schemes:

- **The Property Ombudsman (TPO)** - http://bit.ly/29HKlV5

- **Property Redress Scheme (PRS)** - http://bit.ly/2kskG21

- **Ombudsman Services Guide to Membership** - http://bit.ly/2qIc3UF

Guides

Anti-Money Laundering (AML)

HMRC

- **Registration** - http://bit.ly/2l3sPeX

- **Registration Form** - http://bit.ly/2kslhAz

- **Fees Guide** - http://bit.ly/2j7sMNk

- **Supervision Guide** - http://bit.ly/1mQgib1

- **E-Learning** - http://bit.ly/1HYgU5R

General

- **The Money Laundering Bulletin (Information) –** http://bit.ly/L3m2yu

- **The Journal of Money Laundering Control (Emerald) -** http://bit.ly/2rjtUV4

- **(NFoPP) - Guide to AML** - http://bit.ly/2l3xpdm

- **Joint Money Laundering Steering Group - Guide to AML -** http://bit.ly/1ztNnjT

National Crime Agency (NCA)

- **NCA Site** - http://bit.ly/Rn4BvX

- **NCA Registration** - http://bit.ly/2km84OL

- **NCA – Guide Money Laundering** - http://bit.ly/1Pf9ZgG

- **NCA – SAR's Online System** - http://bit.ly/2lbBEGd

- **NCA – Consent Regime** - http://bit.ly/2kOjGc0

Bribery Act 2010

- **Ministry of Justice Guide to Bribery Act 2010** - http://bit.ly/1fmzCor

- **Government Guide to Bribery Act 2010** - http://bit.ly/1RfRr1k

- **Ministry of Justice Quick Start Guide to Bribery Act 2010** - http://bit.ly/1Hqycbq

Data Protection Act 1998

- **ICO Guide to Data Protection** - http://bit.ly/1MRKU83

- **Information Commissioners Office (ICO) Register** - http://bit.ly/1NfOsP2

- **Information Commissioners Office (ICO) - Registered – What next** - http://bit.ly/2kFRo0L

- **Information Commissioners Office (ICO) - How to Comply Checklist** - http://bit.ly/1sg3pxn

Insurance

- **Health and Safety Executive (HSE) – Guide to Employers Liability Insurance** - http://bit.ly/1Jt7Bep

- **Government Guide to Employees Insurance** - http://bit.ly/1IiLR3X

- **Association of British Insurers (ABI) – Guide for Small Business** - http://bit.ly/2qJYW9J

Client Accounts

- **Client Account: Guide** - http://bit.ly/2lhsOa5

- **RICS: Guide to Client Accounts** - http://bit.ly/1FaQCuD

Consumers, Estate Agents and Redress Act 2007

- **NFoPP Guide to Consumers, Estate Agents and Redress Act 2007** - http://bit.ly/2kmgTYX

Proceeds of Crime Act 2002

- **RICS Guide to Proceeds of Crime Act** - http://bit.ly/2kSBXEK

Consumer Protection Regulations 2008 (CPR's) & Business Protection from Misleading Marketing Regulations 2008 (BPR's)

- **NTSEAT Guide to CPR's** - http://bit.ly/2kK05Hb

- **The Property Ombudsman Interim Report 2013** - http://bit.ly/2ruFDx6

- *RIC's Guide* - *http://bit.ly/2pZIRrl*

- *OFT Guide* - *http://bit.ly/2pOihq1*

Consumer Rights Act 2015

- **Business Companion Guide to Consumer Rights Act 2015** - http://bit.ly/28LgV6D

Companies Act 2006 & Companies Limited Liability Partnerships and Business Regulations 2015

- **Companies House Guide** - http://bit.ly/2l3QUT3

EPC's

- **Government Guide to EPC's** - http://bit.ly/1VYB8WI

- **RICS Guide to EPC's** - http://bit.ly/2l3Krrj

General

- **RICS: Guide for Agents** - http://bit.ly/2lL5oqd

- **NTSEAT: Guide Estate Agents** - http://bit.ly/2l3KEKR

- **Email Alerts: Corruption UK** - http://bit.ly/SOr0TG

- **Office of Fair Trade (OFT): Guide for Estate Agents** - http://bit.ly/2sxh6Ip

Due Diligence Checks

- **HM Treasury Sanctions List: Email Subscription** - http://bit.ly/1uVW0i4

- **FCA: Finance Regulated Companies Check** - http://bit.ly/1pEyzK2

- **Companies House (UK): Company Check** – http://bit.ly/2ksxSDL

- **FAME Database (UK and Ireland): Company Check** - http://bit.ly/2kmhOII

- **Guide to Fame** - http://bit.ly/2l3PwQq

- **AMADEUS database (Europe): Company Checks** - http://bit.ly/1RktGEc

- **European Economic Area (EEA)** - http://bit.ly/1AkUg44

- **HMT Financial Sanctions List** - http://bit.ly/1wC8YSW

- **HMT Financial Sanctions List: Register for Updates** - http://bit.ly/1uVW0i4

- **Charity Commission Register: Charity Checks** - http://bit.ly/1ogsy7N

Electronic checking companies

- **Experian: Authenticate People** - http://bit.ly/1jN26x5

- **Tracesmart (LexisNexis Risk Solutions): High Risk Individual Checks, ID Verification** - http://bit.ly/2lLi7Kl

- **Veriphy: AML, Company and Credit Checks** - http://bit.ly/2l3Nr6Y

- **Accuity: AML, Sanctions, PEP and Transactions Screening** - http://bit.ly/2lFOSLU

- **Equifax: ID Authentication Service (Preferred provider for: The Law Society for PEP and Sanctions Screening)** - http://bit.ly/2kFFnse

Marketing and Presenting:

- **FSA Fact Sheet – Unregulated Collective Investment Schemes (UCIS)** - http://bit.ly/2rCqM4N

- **FCA Guide – Restrictions on Promotions** - http://bit.ly/2s95zm3

- **FCA Guide – Financial Promotion** - http://bit.ly/2qXhjTO

- **FCA Guide – Conduct of Business -** http://bit.ly/2rZsFfb

- **FCA Guide – Financial Promotions in Social Media -** http://bit.ly/2qSvdYj

Outdoor Advertisements:

- **Communities and Local Government – A Guide Outdoor Advertisements and Signs** - http://bit.ly/1Fhw5LO

Let me share with you my vast
industry knowledge and expertise.
You can discover all of our upcoming
events and courses...

EVENTS &
COURSES

Find the latest events and courses at:

www.getpropertycompliant/events-and-courses

I wish you every success with either your
property sourcing business or your investments
in the property sector.

Tina x

Let me know how you're getting on in my
Facebook Group:
PropertySourcingComplianceSupport

Printed in Great Britain
by Amazon

54618577R00099